JAWDROPPERS

36 Shocking Stories for Students
Based on the Sayings of Jesus

STEVEN JAMES

EMPOWERED® Youth Products
Standard Publishing
Cincinnati, Ohio

DEDICATION
To Trinity, Ariel and Eden

SPECIAL THANKS

to all who read and responded to these stories in various forms; to Eddie Brittain for listening, being honest and sharing his tomatoes; to Sonja and Chris Haskins for helping me sharpen my focus; to J. P. Abner for his cheese alerts; to Eddy Hall for telling me I was a writer; to fellow storytellers C. Keith Young, Joe, "Doc" Moore, Aaron Wymer, Bill Noomah and Tracy Radosevic who encouraged me to keep writing; and to the sophomores at Providence Academy for journeying with me into the life of Christ.

All Scripture quotations, unless otherwise indicated, are taken from the HOLY BIBLE, NEW INTER-NATIONAL VERSION®. NIV®. Copyright © 1973, 1978, 1984 by International Bible Society. Used by permission of Zondervan Publishing House. All rights reserved.

Cover photo by The Stock Market/Christian Belpaire
Cover and inside design by Dina Sorn
Edited by Dale Reeves and Leslie Durden

Library of Congress Cataloging-in-Publication Data:
James, Steven, 1969-
    Jawdroppers : 36 shocking stories for students based on the sayings of Jesus / Steven James.
      p. cm.
    Includes indexes.
    ISBN 0-7847-1264-6
    1. Parables--Paraphrases, tales, etc.--Juvenile literature. 2. Jesus
Christ--Parables--Juvenile literature. [1. Jesus Christ--Parables. 2. Parables. 3. Bible
stories--N.T.] I. Title.
BT376.J36 2001
232.9'54--dc21

2001020275

Standard Publishing, Cincinnati, Ohio.
A Division of Standex International Corporation.

08	07	06	05	04	03	02
5	4	3				

ISBN: 0-7847-1264-6

CONTENTS

INTRODUCTION
A PARABLE ABOUT PARABLES

The sign outside the restaurant read, *"Burger Empire: Home of the TruthBurger."*

Hmmm, thought Nate. *Maybe I'll give it a try.* After all, lots of his friends had recommended the place, and he was famished.

A girl about his age was wiping down the counter when he found a seat. Hm. Kinda cute.

"My name is Megan and I'll be your server," she chirped. "Do you know what you want—or do you need a menu?"

"I've heard good things about the TruthBurger," said Nate.

Megan smiled, "It's our specialty."

"All right then! I'd like mine medium-rare."

Megan shook her head, "I'm sorry, well-done is the only way we cook the TruthBurger. But it's 100% Certified USDA Truth. And it's really good for you. Still wanna try it?"

"Sure . . ." he said, rubbing his stomach. "And I'm starved, so why don't you Mongo-size that? Give me the biggest one you've got."

But Megan shook her head. "Um . . . you might want to start with the bite-size TruthBurger. It's really filling and quite nutritious. Some people find the Mongo TruthBurger is a little too much to swallow at first."

Nate looked at her curiously. He'd never heard a server recommend a smaller size meal before! "Okay, whatever," he said.

Megan nodded, tossed her hair to the side and set down a glass of water. "It'll be just a sec."

What a weird place. No pounding music. No flashing lights. No dance floor. No video games . . . just a normal-looking restaurant. He couldn't believe it was so popular with his friends! It didn't look all that special to him.

TruthBurger, huh? Well, we'll see.

A few minutes later, Megan came hurrying back carrying a charred-looking piece of charcoal nestled between two buns.

"That's the TruthBurger?" exclaimed Nate. "It looks like a hockey puck after losing a fight with an arsonist!"

Megan set the plate down. "It may not look great, but wait 'til you taste it!"

Nate stared at the TruthBurger without moving.

"Go on," urged Megan.

Partly because he was so hungry and partly because Megan was so cute, he lifted the TruthBurger to his lips and took a bite.

Ugh!

"Man, this is tough to chew!" said Nate, thinking, *That's the understatement of the century*! "It tastes like it's been cooking forever!"

"Oh, here! I almost forgot!" Megan grabbed a bottle from his table and handed it to him. "You need to put some of this on there. It really brings out the taste!"

"What is it?"

"Parable Sauce."

"Parable Sauce? What's it taste like?"

"Oh, you'll like it. Trust me."

Nate wasn't so sure. What if it only made the TruthBurger taste worse?

But he *was* really hungry. . . . Okay, why not? He squirted some Parable Sauce onto the flame-broiled coal and bit into his TruthBurger once again.

Whoa!

It was unbelievable! Like nothing he'd ever tasted before! Delicious and filling! And juicy and sweet!

Megan smiled, "Nibble! Enjoy yourself! Don't bite off more than you can chew!"

He couldn't believe how much the Parable Sauce helped! "Man, this TruthBurger is *incredible* with that Parable Sauce stuff! It's amazing how well they go together!"

"Yeah. Most people think Parable Sauce isn't very filling by itself, but when you pour some on one of our TruthBurgers—it's a winning combination."

"I'll say!"

Nate finished his TruthBurger, tipped Megan generously and knew he'd be back again. Soon.

And when he left Burger Empire that day, he wasn't hungry anymore.

"With many similar parables Jesus spoke the word to them, as much as they could understand. He did not say anything to them without using a parable" (Mark 4:33, 34).

Chomp. Chomp.

Jesus knew the tastiest way to serve up truth was with a little story. But the stories Jesus told weren't warm-n-fuzzy, feely-good fairy tales where everyone lived happily ever after. In his stories people got beat up, imprisoned, tortured, killed and even sliced into little pieces. The good guy sometimes lost. Hard work didn't always pay off. And things were not always what they appeared to be.

His stories were shockers. Parables with a knockout punch. They carried enough force to change the way his listeners looked at life forever, shaking people out of their comfort zones and into the kingdom of Heaven.

Jesus wanted to wake people up and get them thinking about their relationship with God in a new and fresh way. So Jesus told *Jawdroppers*.

And it worked. People listened with amazement, shock, confusion, delight . . . and anger. Even if they didn't like his message, they couldn't resist listening to it. The stories would sneak in, fly under their radar and hit 'em with a fistful of truth right between the eyes.

Get ready to revisit Jesus' stories. Prepare to take a fresh look at what he had to say. It's time to sink your teeth in and savor a bite of truth for yourself. But beware—sometimes truth bites back.

Enjoy your meal.

1

REBELLION ON TERRA 5

Ambassador Lansing gripped the throttle and jerked his ship back on course. The flight computers were off-line and he hadn't flown manually since he was at the academy. To make matters worse, the ship had been heavily damaged in his escape.

C'mon! C'mon! You can make it!

Up ahead he saw Phoenix Station quickly approaching. It wouldn't be long now.

C'mon, baby. Ease in there . . . just a little further . . .

The rear thrusters finally disengaged and his pod began to slow down. He veered sharply toward the left side of Docking Bay 12-C7. He knew he was coming in way too fast, but he didn't have a choice. Not this time.

No . . . It's not right! . . . The trajectory is too steep!

Everything was getting foggy for the ambassador. He'd lost too much blood. And he was so dizzy—dizziness was one of the symptoms of the Demarian Plague. He'd most certainly been infected. If only he could make it into the docking bay to deliver his message!

He heard the warning blaring from the com device near his ear, but it was too late. As the ship careened wildly to the side, everything seemed to blur together like a dream. Like a nightmare.

You're not gonna make it! You've failed. The Emperor will lose the colonies. . . .

The last thing he saw before his ship exploded in a flash of light was the metal exterior of the space station zooming toward him.

● ●

"Sir? Sir? Can you hear me?"

The man lying on the operating table blinked his eyes.

"Your Majesty, I believe he's coming to!" said Dr. Exeter, Phoenix Station's chief physician. He leaned over Ambassador Lansing's body, prodding gently at the artificial limbs he'd just attached.

The Emperor stepped forward. "Excellent. That'll be all, doctor. You may leave us alone now." Dr. Exeter nodded, bowed twice and quietly backed out of the room.

"What? Where am I?" mumbled the ambassador. "What happened?"

"We pulled you from a nasty wreck, my friend. But the good doctor found enough of you to piece back together. . . ." The Emperor smiled. "By the way, you dented my space station, Ambassador."

The man on the table closed his eyes. "My life for my mistake, Your Majesty."

"No, no. I forgive you. . . ." The Emperor leaned close and lowered his voice to a whisper. "Now, tell me about those burns on your leg and how your right foot came to be severed from your body. . . . It wasn't from the wreck, was it?"

There was a long and uncomfortable silence.

"Ambassador?"

"No, sir. It wasn't from the wreck. I was tortured. It was the rebels."

The Emperor's eyes narrowed. "The rebels did this to you? To my personal representative!"

"They refused to listen to anything I had to say, and wouldn't hand over the antitoxin. They're trying to keep it all to themselves, sir."

"And what about the others—Ambassador Lege? Dr. Akersby? Sir Magel, the Honorable Envoy from Nebus?"

"Dead, sir. I was the only one to escape. . . . I had to gnaw off my thumbs to twist my hands out of the shackles."

The Emperor turned on his heels. "You serve me well and you will be rewarded for your loyalty. We'll speak again soon. For now, rest. I have much to think about. I need to speak with my counselor."

Ambassador Lansing bent his head slightly and glanced at his new thumbs. *Better than the originals*, he thought, as the dizziness returned. And then he was asleep again.

• •

Four earth hours later, he awoke in a hoverchair. Dr. Exeter was guiding him down the corridor toward the Emperor's High Chamber.

Counselor Pax and the Emperor's son, Lucan, were already assembled in the council room. The Emperor motioned for them to sit down. Then he turned toward Ambassador Lansing. "Thank you for joining us on such short notice, Ambassador. Could you give us a status report of the rebellion on Terra 5?"

"Of course, sir." He propped himself up with his arms and addressed the three dignitaries. "The rebels have taken control of the plantations that produce the antitoxin for Demarian Plague. . . ." He glanced at Dr. Exeter.

The doctor looked grim as he added to the ambassador's report. "As you all know, it's highly contagious and . . . quite fatal, I'm afraid. Everyone in the Terra System has been exposed."

Ambassador Lansing swallowed hard. That "everyone" included him. He cleared his throat and continued. "They've refused to turn over the antitoxin. Every messenger that's been sent has been killed or tortured. . . . As I see it, Your Majesty, we have only one choice. . . ." There really was only one option left—send in a squadron of Elite Force soldiers. Annihilate the rebels, seize the antitoxin and then distribute it throughout the colonies.

But before he could propose this, Counselor Pax cleared his throat. "I suggest you send in Prince Lucan."

"What?" roared the Emperor. "My son? My only son! You propose I send the one I love more than anyone else to those murderous rebels?"

Prince Lucan stepped forward. "I'm glad to go, Dad. The antitoxin can save whole worlds. Billions of people—your people. I'd gladly lay down my life for them. . . ."

Counselor Pax spoke up again. "Certainly the rebels will respect your only son, sir. And then this entire incident can be resolved peacefully. They wouldn't dare attack the son of their Emperor. Lucan will arrive in an unarmed ship. No weapons. Bringing only your undeserved offer of mercy."

The Emperor gazed around the room. "What do you think, Ambassador?"

Ambassador Lansing shook his head. "Sir, I don't see the wisdom in it. Knowing the rebels, they'll try to assassinate your son. They'll reason

11

that if they can kill the heir to the throne, the entire galaxy will be theirs. I suggest an Elite Force offensive instead."

Everyone stared at the Emperor awaiting his command. A long moment passed. Then another. "Thank you, Ambassador. Your suggestion is duly noted. But this time I must go with Counselor Pax's proposal." He drew a deep breath, and, despite himself, the Emperor clenched his fists in intensity. "But if they lay a hand on Lucan, I will bring them all to a wretched end. By peace or by force, the antitoxin will be taken from them and entrusted to those who'll share it willingly with others, rather than keep it only to themselves."

Ambassador Lansing couldn't believe it. *This is unheard of! Never has an emperor allowed his only son to enter enemy territory in the middle of an uprising! He could be captured! Or even killed!*

"When shall I leave, Father?"

"At once. Time is of the essence."

"But, Your Majesty!" blurted the ambassador. "It's a suicide mission!"

"Perhaps," said the Emperor. "But love will prevail in the end. It's the only way to save the planet. It's the only way to save . . . you."

Prince Lucan turned toward the ambassador. "I'll be back," he said, laying his hand on the ambassador's shoulder. "And I will bring you the antitoxin. I promise."

Then Lucan nodded to his father and the others, removed his royal sash and robes, laid his weapons on the table and left the room to save Terra 5.

From itself.

CHECK IT OUT...

Do you think the prince was successful? Read Mark 12:1-9 to find out how the story ends. Notice how the rebels treated the son when he arrived.

THINK IT OUT...

Jesus told this story to upstanding, well-respected Bible scholars who'd done two things—(1) repeatedly ignored God's messages to them, and (2) tried to keep God's blessings to themselves.

God won't put up with that kind of an attitude (see verses 9-11). Don't let those verses apply to you.

There's a surprisingly simple way to discover if you truly love God: How do you respond when you hear one of his commands? Do you make excuses and rationalize about the lifestyle you've chosen, or do you look for ways to begin obeying what God has said? Do you share the blessings of knowing God with others, or do you keep the message to yourself?

LIVE IT OUT...

Servant after servant went into the vineyard, knowing what had happened to the others. Torture. Beatings. Death. Why did they go? They went because they loved the orchard owner. And their love compelled them to obey. Are you more like those servants who were willing to die for their master, or the rebels who refused to acknowledge his authority?

Sure, we all mess up and make mistakes. But, what attitude do you have toward God's messengers? One of rebellion? Or one of submission? True obedience starts in the heart. What changes in attitude and action does God want you to make today?

PRAY IT OUT...

God, I'm tempted to make excuses, ignore your commands and keep the news of your love to myself—just like the rebels did. Forgive me! Help me to be more like the servants and less like the rebels. You want me to share the blessings of knowing you with other people. That means telling people about Jesus. Give me the guts to do it. Not out of obligation, but out of love. Amen.

2

WHEN THE FITNESS MOVEMENT CAME TO TOWN

Before the Fitness Movement came to town, I would never have considered myself "out of shape." Sure, I'd gained a few pounds here and there. Sure, I watched a little TV when I could have been out running or cross-country skiing. Sure, I had my share of sweet rolls and chocolate cake, but who didn't? And besides, I was in much better shape than *most* people.

But when the Fitness Movement came to town, the Fitness Recruiter told us that everybody needs to exercise. He said that you can't be truly fit unless you eat the right food. "You are what you eat," he told us. "Whatever you pour down your throat is what you become. Finally, friends, whatever is natural, whatever is healthy, whatever is organic, whatever is wholesome, whatever is hygienic, whatever is homogenized—if anything is low in saturated fats or cholesterol—devour such things."

He told us to exercise regularly and train diligently. "I was once like you," he said, "chubby, flabby, out of shape. But then I started to exercise every day and eat the right kinds of food. The Fitness Manual changed my life! In it you'll find all you ever need to know about healthy eating and exercise, and you can read about the Greatest Athlete of all! Read through the pages of this book and you'll never be the same person again! No longer do I view myself as just another couch potato or lounge lizard. I realize I'm one of his team members, and you can be, too!"

Well, a bunch of us started to gather and discuss the Fitness Movement. Every day we would meet together in the tennis courts. Finally, we moved our meetings to the Gym, to read the Fitness Manual and exercise together. We didn't care what kind of background a person had, we were just happy to have him there, exercising with us. One person was a music teacher, so she played the organ while the rest of us did aerobics together.

Sometimes people got up and shared how their lives had been changed since they heard about the Greatest Athlete of all and became Athletes themselves. I still remember the day I got up to share my story. I was so nervous and scared!

"I used to sit and watch TV every day," I told those sitting on the locker-room benches. "I'd fill my face with apple pies covered with whipped cream, triple-decker cherry-chocolate cakes with extra frosting, cream-filled donuts and sweet rolls. . . . Once in a while I'd eat some nice sizzling bacon and scrambled eggs for breakfast."

A series of gasps went up from my astonished listeners. "Not you!" I heard someone say.

"Yes, it's true," I said. "I shudder to think of my old lifestyle. But not anymore!" I held up my worn copy of the Fitness Manual. "Now, things are different. I can run and not grow weary! I can walk and not be faint! My old body is gone. My new body is here!" Cheers went up from those in the Gymnasium. It was like a pep rally; we all jumped rope for a while and then did pull-ups while the music teacher played a chorus of "Amazing Race."

Yeah, that's how things were at the beginning. But since then, things have changed.

It didn't happen all at once. A secret bag of chips here, a skipped workout there. I began to notice that I wasn't as excited to hear about the Greatest Athlete of all anymore. Everyone said he'd be coming to town soon, but he never showed up. Some of those in the Gym began to doubt there really was a Greatest Athlete of all. Others began to complain that the workouts were too difficult for beginning Athletes. Some said the Gym was too large and noisy. Others complained that it was too cold in the winter and too hot in the summer. Several people left the Gym because they didn't like the music. Finally, we decided to change things so people would feel more welcome.

First, we carpeted the locker room and replaced the old benches with comfortable recliners. Next went the workouts. No longer did *we* actually break into a sweat. Instead, we hired a really gifted Athlete to stand up front and exercise while we watched. It sure made the meetings a lot easier. There were no more twisted ankles, no more sweaty towels to wash, no broken equipment to fix.

The third thing to go was the music teacher. We figured we didn't actually need someone there *playing* the music; it was much cheaper to buy CDs and pop them into the boom box.

Then we changed the name. Instead of calling our Gym a "Fitness Center," we named it "The Health Club." That has a nice ring to it, don't you think? And that's what it's more like these days, anyhow—a club.

Finally, we dropped the readings from the Fitness Manual. After all, some people got offended by what was written in there. Some people didn't like the idea that the Manual covered only certain sports and not their favorites—like darts and chess. Others found a typo on page 1019. They said, "Any book filled with mistakes and contradictions isn't reliable." Some got bored with the readings, and some just felt guilty for being so out of shape. After all, the Manual taught about how perfect the Greatest Athlete of all was, and how flabby we all are. And those lists of Athletes from the past! Ugh!

That's when I stopped supporting the Athletic Fund which helped to train Fitness Recruiters and supply copies of the Fitness Manual to people in other countries. "There are lots of ways to stay fit," I reasoned. "Who's to say one sport is better than another?"

I started going to the workouts just to be seen by the other Athletes. Even though I was putting on a little weight again, nobody really noticed because I still dressed, talked and acted like a committed Athlete.

Sometimes when I went to the Gym I'd feel guilty about not exercising as much anymore. So I'd promise myself that I'd lift weights again soon or pull out my old rollerblades next week. But I never seemed to get around to it.

When people asked me how my workouts were going, I'd suck in my gut and explain that I just hadn't had time to exercise lately but that I was thinking about going on a diet again and entering another race next year.

When I first became an Athlete, I used to exercise every day! Can you imagine! That *is* a little much, don't you think? I mean, I wouldn't want people to think I was an athletic fanatic, or anything! And besides, I was in such good shape that I figure I can go for a while without exercising. An hour a week should be enough. Huh, my girlfriend works out three times a week! That oughtta be enough for both of us!

Occasionally, I still replace the shoelaces in my sneakers, or buy some new piece of Gym equipment for my basement, or drink diet soda or pass up thirds for dessert. I feel better for a while, but then I get depressed and start right back in again eating meals between my snacks.

Nope, I'm not a regular at the Club anymore—it's just too far of a walk to get there.

But I still have my membership card! That oughtta count for something! And I still have my Fitness Manual on the shelf somewhere. Maybe I'll read it tomorrow. Yeah, that's it, I'll search through my books and dig out that old dusty thing and flip through it. Tomorrow.

But for right now . . . I wonder what's on TV.

CHECK IT OUT...

Jesus loved to tell stories that shook people up. He wanted them to think about their relationship with God in a new way. Read Jesus' story of the four soils told in Luke 8:4-15. Sometimes his stories hit a little too close to home.

THINK IT OUT...

To God there are no losers, only quitters. Have you ever felt like dropping out? What are your favorite excuses for not growing closer to God? Which ones do you use over and over? Why are they so easy to keep using? How do you fake it when you aren't really walking the talk?

Which of those soils are you most like? What about the guy who joined the Fitness Movement—which one is he like? At what point in the story could you identify with him most closely? When he was:

- an interested bystander?
- on fire for his new lifestyle?
- full of excuses for his lack of growth?
- pretending to be committed when the fire was gone?
- back to being spiritually flabby?

LIVE IT OUT...

Have you joined the real Fitness Movement? If so, are you making choices that are spiritually healthy, or have you become a spiritual couch potato? It's easy to get distracted and lose steam. Don't let things like laziness, worry, money or the pursuit of pleasure detour you from maturing in your faith! This week, pull out your copy of the Fitness Manual and commit to getting your spiritual life back on track!

PRAY IT OUT...

God, you know where I am. You know what my attitude has been. Forgive me for not always taking my commitment to you seriously. Open up ways for me to grow closer to you, and give me the guts to say "yes" to you, even when it means making tough choices. I want to run the race for you every day, even when I'm out of breath. Thanks, God, for listening. Amen.

3

A Tale of Two Sons

Jake's dad called him and his brother Eddie into the living room.

"Now, boys," their father began, "you both know what the Bible says about premarital sex. I don't want to get preachy or anything, but I'd like you to promise me you'll avoid situations where you might be tempted to do something you'd later regret." He paused to make sure he had their undivided attention. "Do you promise to stay sexually pure until you get married?"

Eddie snickered. "Whatever! Listen, Dad, I'll do what I want, all right? I mean, if God invented sex and it's supposed to be so great, why would he tell us we can't do it? And another thing, I'm tired of you telling me what I should and shouldn't do. I'm outta here!" Eddie stood up and stormed out of the living room.

Jake stared at his brother. How could he talk to Dad that way? Jake couldn't believe it! Then again, maybe he could. Eddie *had* always been sort of a rebel, purposely doing the opposite of whatever Dad said. Breaking the rules. Breaking the law. He'd even been picked up for shoplifting a couple of times! Jake expected his dad to yell or something. But he didn't. He just mumbled, "Do what you have to do, Eddie."

Jake turned to his father. "Sure, Dad. No problem. I promise *I'll* do just as you ask."

And Jake followed through. He kept his promise. He helped form a *True Love Waits* group at his high school and wrote editorials for his school paper. And when anyone asked, he openly shared that he was gonna remain a virgin until he got married. As president of First Community Church's youth group, he helped counsel other students away from sexual pressures. Everyone knew where Jake stood and they respected him for it.

Eddie, on the other hand, wasted no time. He'd only been seeing Cherise for a week when he pressured her to sleep with him. She hesitated at first, but then gave in and told herself it was no big deal. And, when word leaked out that she was pregnant, no one was surprised. After all, Eddie wasn't the first boy she'd been with. The students at their school had a name for girls like her.

Jake wasn't surprised either. He'd always expected as much out of his brother. And neither was he surprised when Eddie dropped out of high school and got a job working as a mechanic. And then, when Cherise moved in with him and they started renting a trailer on the edge of town, Jake couldn't help but think, "What a loser! What a disgrace to our family name!"

Sure, Jake went to visit them at the trailer park few times, but he always felt uncomfortable being there because they were . . . well . . . living together . . . and they weren't even married. "Maybe it'd be best if I just ignored them for awhile," he thought. "Maybe then they'll feel guilty enough to change."

A few months later, when the baby was born, Eddie and Cherise started attending church again. But Jake didn't notice. He'd gone on to attend a small Bible college upstate on an academic scholarship.

He was so busy at college—with planning campus ministry events and working part-time at the mall—that he didn't have time to think about his wayward brother. He barely had enough time to keep his GPA up!

Then, one day, Jake met Jena.

She worked in the library, and one night she invited him over to her room to study. Their study sessions went later and later until one night he didn't make it home until breakfast. A few weeks later, she e-mailed him with the news—she was expecting.

This was terrible! Jake knew he could never face his dad or his friends, especially since he'd been so outspoken about sexual purity. He knew right away what he had to do.

Jake quickly gave Jena the $300 she said she needed to "get it taken care of." He figured this way no one would ever find out—no sense ruining his reputation over one little mistake. He and Jena went out a few more times, but things just didn't work out. They broke up and Jake went on to graduate at the top of his class. And then it was off to seminary. No one was ever the wiser.

And now, all these years later, Eddie and Cherise are still living in that trailer. Eddie went on to get his GED and hopes to one day own that garage where he works. Their son, Billy Joe, just turned six years old. He loves watching wrestling on TV, helping his daddy work on cars and going to the park with Grandpa.

And Jake?

Well, he hasn't been back home to visit in awhile. And he keeps forgetting to drop Dad a note. After all, he's serving as the pastor at a big church in another state.

And that keeps him awfully busy.

CHECK IT OUT...

Jesus loved to shatter stereotypes. The "church" people of his time thought they were shoo-ins for Heaven because of their perfect church attendance and long religious heritage. But they neglected doing the two things God requires for admission into his kingdom. Read Matthew 21:28-32 (especially the last part of verse 32) to find out what those two things are.

THINK IT OUT...

Which of the two brothers was more successful? Why?

Does it seem fair that Jake lived such a good life (except for one little mistake) yet ended up looking like such a loser? What was the thing that was *really* wrong with his life? Isn't "being good" what Christianity is all about?

Nope. It's not. Christianity is about those two things in verse 32—faith and repentance. Repentance means changing your mind and turning in a new direction. Faith means trusting in something that you can't even see. That's why Jesus said crooks and prostitutes are getting into Heaven in front of all those nice, friendly, upstanding churchgoing people—because they'd repented and placed their faith in God while the "religious" people hadn't.

LIVE IT OUT...

Which brother repented? Which one didn't? Have *you* ever really repented?

Don't play games with God. He isn't looking for people who look good on the outside. He isn't impressed by church attendance, youth group involvement or how many Bible verses you can recite. It's what's in your heart that matters to him. Even if you've done terrible, regrettable things, he'll forgive you. Heaven's doors are open wide to all who repent and believe.

PRAY IT OUT...

Dear Jesus, sometimes I look down on the lifestyles of others. I judge them and think they're worse than me. But you look into the heart. Even those with a checkered past are welcome in Heaven when they turn to you and believe. Today, I'd like to let go of those things that have kept me from following you with all of my heart. I trust in you, Jesus. I turn to you. I rely on you. I won't pretend any longer. You know my heart, and today I give all of myself to you. Amen.

4

TIME FOR POPCORN

Randy just shook his head. "I'm not bringing him, Mom! *I am not gonna bring my bratty little brother along on a date!*"

But Randy's mom just grabbed her car keys from the countertop. "The babysitter got sick and I have a PTA meeting. There's no other choice. You're taking him along or you're calling that sweet little honey of yours on the phone and telling her you can't take her out tonight."

"Mom! You can't do this to me!"

"Sure I can. Dennis can watch the movie with you." Then she turned to Randy's little brother Dennis. "You'll be good, won't you, Dennis?"

Dennis grinned and nodded.

"Oh, great," said Randy.

"It's settled, then. I have to go. Say 'hi' to Kiera for me." She gave each of her boys a quick peck on the cheek and disappeared out the door.

Dennis ran over to his big brother. "This is gonna be fun, Randy! Will you buy me some popcorn? Huh? Please? Huh? I love popcorn so much! Can we get some popcorn on our date?"

Randy leaned over and got right in his little brother's face. "Listen to me, it's not *our* date. It's *my* date. And the only reason I'm bringing you along is because Mom told me I have to. You're sitting in the backseat and not a peep. Understand me?"

"Okay. But can I have some popcorn?"

"No."

Randy herded his little brother into the car and drove over to pick up Kiera. The whole way Dennis kept asking for popcorn. "Please! Please! Please! Pretty please with sugar and honey and ice cream and gumballs on top?"

"Would you please shut up!" Randy yelled. Then he just shook his head and mumbled to himself. "This is gonna be a long night."

When he got to Kiera's house, Randy explained everything. "My mom told me I had to bring him along."

She smiled and waved at Dennis in the backseat. "Oh, it's okay! Your little brother is so cute!"

"He's not cute."

"I just wanna reach out and give him a hug."

"Oh, brother." He slipped behind the wheel and they headed to Wally's Drive-In.

"Please can we get some popcorn? Please! I love popcorn!"

"No!"

As they pulled into their place and the movie started, Randy leaned toward Kiera. Kiera leaned toward Randy and just as they turned to gaze into each other's eyes, there was a face between them. "I like it with extra butter."

"Ah!" screamed Randy. Then he had an idea. "Hey, Dennis, how about Kiera and I sit in the backseat?" He winked at Kiera. "And you can sit up here so you can see the movie better."

"Okay, Randy. Can I use the cup holder for my popcorn?"

They switched places and Randy and Kiera began to snuggle up close.

Randy was so distracted he didn't notice that Dennis had begun to explore all the knobs and buttons on the dashboard. He poked and pulled and beeped the horn.

"What was that?" yelled Randy.

"Just me," said Dennis. "That's the hungry horn. Means I'm ready for my popcorn now."

"You're not getting any popcorn! Now watch the movie!"

Randy and Kiera went back to snuggling and Dennis adjusted the mirrors so he could watch his big brother kissing his girlfriend in the backseat. "Yuck," he said.

Then, he found the four-way flashers.

Blink, blink. Blink, blink. Blink, blink.

"Quit that!" said Randy.

Blink, blink. Blink, blink. Blink, blink.

"Turn those things off!"

"Only if you buy me some popcorn."

Blink, blink. Blink, blink. Blink, blink.

"Okay! Okay! I give up! Here! Take my wallet! Go and buy yourself some stinking popcorn! Knock yourself out! Anything to shut you up!"

Dennis's eyes became as big as the steering wheel as he took the money. "Thanks, Randy!"

He slipped out of the car and left Randy and Kiera alone.

"Now, where were we?" whispered Randy. He leaned over to kiss Kiera when the back door opened up.

"Can I get some Junior Mints, too? And maybe a little soda?"

Randy sighed. "Get anything you want."

Dennis grinned. "Oh, goody."

Kiera smiled. "He's so cute!"

"He's not cute."

A few minutes later, Dennis returned with his arms full of treats, including a giant bin of hot, buttery popcorn.

"I bought you two some candy!" he said. "Here!"

And after the movie, Randy dropped Kiera off and went home. His mom was already back.

Dennis ran up to her right away. "Mommy, Mommy! Randy bought me some popcorn!"

She smiled. "Well, that was very nice of you, Randy."

Randy just shook his head and trudged upstairs to get ready for bed while Dennis and his mother finished up the rest of the popcorn.

CHECK IT OUT...

Jesus talked a lot about prayer. He even told two stories about how persistent we should be when we talk to God: the stories of "The Annoying Friend" (Luke 11:1-13) and "The Nagging Lady" (Luke 18:1-8).

The twist in both stories is that the requests were granted for the *wrong* reasons. Why did the judge grant the request? What about the sleepy guy? Why did he hand over his loaf of bread?

Jesus' point is: if they granted the requests for the wrong reasons, won't God—whose reasons are always right—grant our requests?

Duh! Of course!

THINK IT OUT...

How persistent are you? Do you ask God for something just once and then stop? Why? Maybe you've been thinking, "that person is beyond saving," or "since God's been silent for so long, he must want me to stop asking for this thing." Do you give up when you don't get an immediate answer? What might God be trying to teach you by not answering right away?

It's not a sign of unbelief to keep coming to God with the same request over and over and over. It's actually a sign of *faith*.

LIVE IT OUT...

How desperate and persistent were the widow, the friend and Dennis? What does that tell you about your prayers?

Persistent prayers show that we're refusing to give up hope or doubt for a moment that God will answer our requests. So, no matter how long it takes or how unbelievable it may seem, keep on asking. God wants you to make a nuisance out of yourself by coming again and again and again. Always trust that he is listening and an answer is on the way.

Think of something or someone you've given up on or stopped praying for. Go to God right now. Be persistent. Never give up. It'll pay off. You have Jesus' word on it. Guaranteed.

PRAY IT OUT

Okay, God, here's the thing. My prayers haven't been all too persistent, insistent or consistent. But I know you're fair, you're just and you're listening. Help me to trust that you'll answer me even when you don't do it according to my timetable. There's a person I really care about and I'd like to lift him (her) up to you in prayer right now. And I'm not gonna give up, no matter how long it takes. I'm gonna pray with persistence. Like the lady and the man and Dennis. I'll be back again. I promise. Amen.

5

BIG PLANS

10:20 A.M.

Jana Belmont glanced into the rearview mirror, turned the key and backed out of the driveway. It was hard to see out the back of the car because of all the stuff packed in.

College. She was finally on her way to college.

It was almost unbelievable. She'd worked so hard for this. Waited so long. All the tests. All the late nights. All the sacrifices, finally paying off.

A full scholarship to Yale. And she'd earned it.

That, and she'd just landed a modeling job for a major New York magazine. Things were ready to take off.

"Let everyone else laugh now," she thought. "There's no stopping Jana Belmont."

Of course, no one had been laughing at her. Not for a long time. They'd been admiring her. She was the hometown sweetheart, winning all those pageants, getting all those awards.

Yeah, Jana had big plans.

And winning the Miss America Pageant was just one of them.

10:24 A.M.

As she signaled a left-hand turn and crossed the corner in front of the gas station on the end of her block, she remembered back to last spring.

For awhile it had looked like there might be some problems getting the scholarship at Yale. Someone at the admissions office had misplaced some of her paperwork and no one could find it. At the time, some of her friends had encouraged her to just forget about the Ivy League and attend a local Christian college with them.

She'd smiled and nodded and told them she'd consider it. But it just didn't fit into her plans, you know? She needed a major university degree behind her if she was ever gonna make the kind of money she wanted.

Maybe someday she would try out religion. After she'd lived her life for awhile, made it in the world. Then, once she was married and settled down somewhere she could take her kids to church and teach them to be respectable citizens and good, morally upright people.

But then, the paperwork went through and she just put the whole thing out of her mind.

"Yale, here I come," she said to herself.

Besides, you're only young once! You need to enjoy yourself while you can. Make every day count.

10:27 A.M.

She eased onto the highway and aimed the car in the direction of the interstate. There was a lot of traffic on the road, students heading to college, parents returning from summer vacations. But that didn't really bother her. She was on her way to college. To her future.

10:29 A.M.

She turned on the radio and smiled. Life was good. Things were right on track. Everything was going according to plan.

10:32 A.M.

Impact.

10:39 A.M.

The ambulance arrived, but there was nothing the paramedics could do. They said she died on impact. It was quick and painless.

One of the paramedics shook his head. "Sure is a lot of stuff scattered here on the highway," he said, surveying the accident.

"Yeah, looks like she was on her way to college," said his partner.

The first guy sighed. "Poor girl. That truck just came out of nowhere. She never even saw it coming."

And they packed up their things and went home.

Time of death—10:32 A.M.

Arrival in Hell—10:32 A.M.

CHECK IT OUT...

Wait a minute! It's not supposed to end like that! Is it? She can't just die at the end! She worked hard! She had big plans!

That's right. It's not supposed to end like that. For any of us. But it ends like that for too many of us.

People put off thinking about death. They think they'll have years and years to spend (or waste) their lives doing anything they like. But we're not guaranteed a long life. We're not even guaranteed the next breath!

Read Luke 12:13-21. What did all that money do for the rich man?

THINK IT OUT...

Jesus said we should be on our guard against "all kinds" of greed. So obviously there must be more than one kind. The world says, "Indulge yourself!" "Satisfy your urges!" "Go for broke!"

Jesus says, "Watch out!"

Name your favorite flavor of greed: pleasure, extravagance, luxury, envy, jealousy, resentment, lust, a craving for more and more and more. . . . Which one sounds most harmless to you?

LIVE IT OUT...

No matter how sweet they taste, they're all poisonous. And infectious. And deadly. Because they make it seem like there are things other than God that'll make you happy. Or bring fulfillment. Or make life worthwhile.

What's your perspective like? What's tugging at your heart—fame and fortune, or Jesus?

PRAY IT OUT...

Dear God, stuff fills my life. Stuff I own. Stuff I want. Dreams of stuff I'll someday buy. I'm even caught fantasizing about stuff I know I shouldn't have. And it's easy to lose sight of you when all I see is all this stuff. Forgive me for my stuff-centeredness. Help me be centered on you. Nothing else. I wanna be rich toward you and poor toward the things of this world. Undistract me, God. Focus my eyes on Jesus and my life on service. I don't wanna end up like the girl who never saw it coming. Amen.

6

WELCOME TO PINKVILLE

I'll never forget the first time I drove into Pinkville. I mean, I'd heard stories about the place, but I had no idea things would be this bad.

I'd been transferred and my new job required me to relocate. I was really psyched because this new job was something I'd always wanted to do—something I really believed in. I guess you could say it was my dream job!

At first I thought I was gonna be sent to Pasadena, California, but I ended up in Pinkville instead.

Pinkville, of all places.

The most isolated little town in the whole state. Wait, isolated isn't really the word for it. Remote. Secluded. Alien is more like it. And weird. Very weird.

I'm not sure which came first, the name or the town, but for whatever reason, everything in Pinkville is the same color.

Three guesses what color that is and the first two don't count.

Yup. At first when you drive over the mountains and enter the valley, you think maybe it's your eyes playing tricks on you, or the angle of the sunlight coming over the mountains. But then, after a few minutes, you realize it's true. Everything is pink. The houses. The cars. The streets. The food.

And pink is the only color people wear—pink shoes, pink socks, pink shirts and pants and dresses and hats. Pink belts and ties and earrings and scarves. People called "pink rockers" listen to pink music, have pink haircuts and have pink tattoos splattered across their arms. Everywhere you go, you see signs that say, "Think pink!"

Like I said, very weird.

It's like you've suddenly landed on another planet. At first you feel like, "Who cares? I'll just do my own thing. You know; go against the flow. This is a free country. I'll wear any color I want to wear!"

So that's what I did. I wore my blue jeans, a faded yellow baseball cap and my brown leather jacket. I tried out purple and green, orange and red. I even wore mauve. You should have seen the looks people gave me! Like I was crazy or something!

And you know what happened? People shook their heads at me. They walked the other direction. They pointed. They snickered and whispered. And sometimes they even laughed in my face.

But even worse, they began to ignore me. Doors swung shut as I passed. Servers refused to seat me in restaurants. Day after day. Week after week. I was terribly lonely.

And, you know, after awhile, a person gets tired of standing out in the crowd all the time. You want to start fitting in.

So finally, I figured I'd just go ahead and wear a pink tie. You know, like they say, "When in Rome, do as the Romans do."

When in Pinkville, wear pink.

People started noticing me. And talking to me. It was way cool.

Within a week I'd picked out a new set of pink clothes. I started thinking, *Hm . . . pink doesn't look all that bad. I could get used to this.* So it wasn't long before I got rid of all my old colored clothes.

And now? Well, I guess, it's not so bad wearing pink every day. It's got its advantages. I mean, you're always color-coordinated, you don't have to worry about finding things that match and, well, you fit in everywhere you go. That's the important thing, I guess. Fitting in.

Of course, I did lose my job—it's pretty tough managing a greenhouse here. I suppose I could move and look for a greenhouse job somewhere else, but I don't think I will. It was a dumb job anyway. And besides, I kinda like it here. I think I'll stay right here in Pinkville where I fit in. Where I belong.

After all, I wouldn't want to end up someplace weird.

CHECK IT OUT...

Jesus revealed truth by concealing it in stories. A third of Jesus' teachings are stories. His only recorded sermon—the Sermon on the Mount—can be told in less than 20 minutes and is packed with images of salt, light, kingdoms, treasures, sawdust, snakes, fruit and storms. Read part of this sermon for yourself in Matthew 5:13-16.

THINK IT OUT...

Is there anything wrong with wanting to fit in? When doesn't it please God? What do you think it means to "lose your saltiness"? Have you ever seen that happen to anyone? What are some of the ways that someone can "let his light shine"?

Jesus had every opportunity to "sell out." What if he'd just given up on this whole "Savior-of-the-world" thing and gotten married, had kids and settled down in a seaside condo there in Galilee? Come to think of it, why didn't he? (See Hebrews 12:2.)

LIVE IT OUT...

The last thing Jesus did was fit in. He didn't act like the religious leaders of his day, he didn't talk like them, he didn't even hang out with them. And they rejected him for it. Big time.

We all like to fit in. But when "fitting in" means compromising what you believe in or value most, it's never worth it. Compromise happens little by little until you start giving up the things that are truly important. Jesus wouldn't give in. Neither should we. This week, think of three things you can do to let your light shine, and point people back to the true source of light. And remember—what's cool with your friends isn't necessarily pleasing to God.

PRAY IT OUT...

God, I'm gonna be honest with you—it's so hard to go against the flow, to stand out in a crowd. Being accepted seems so important and winning the approval of my friends is so attractive. Help me stand up for what I believe in, even when it means standing alone. That's what you did, and that's what you've called me to do to. Give me the boldness to never be ashamed, intimidated or embarrassed to be one of your followers. I wanna become more like Jesus and less like the people who surround me every day. Shine your light through me. Amen.

7

CODE NAME: WOLF

A light gray car zipped down the long winding road to the main entrance of St. Andrew's Nuclear Power Plant. Up ahead, a cruelly-curved barbwire fence stretched 12 feet into the air and two heavily armed guards stood at attention. As the car slowed, both guards leveled their weapons at the driver and a computerized voice threatened, *"Identify yourself immediately!"*

"Colonel Carter Anderson," said the man in the car. "I have a meeting with General Watson tonight."

"Prepare for retinal scan," replied the voice.

The man leaned his head out the window and a mesh of red laser sensors zipped across his eyes.

A green light flashed on the turret and the gate slowly eased open. The two guards lowered their guns and saluted. The man in the car nodded and returned their salute as he rolled past. The metal gate swung shut behind him.

For a moment, he gazed in the rearview mirror to make sure he wasn't being targeted by the automatic tracking system. Nope. The gate was already shut. Everything looked good. He smiled to himself. Whew. So far, so good. His supervisors hadn't said anything about retinal scans. Good thing he'd been prepared.

He lit a cigarette and puffed it gently.

Of course, the real Colonel Anderson would never have smoked in the car. He didn't smoke at all. According to his file, he had never smoked.

And now, of course, he would never get the chance.

His body had been needed for the disguise. At first the surgeons thought they'd just need his eyeballs, teeth and skin for the identity transfer. But, by the time they were done with him, there wasn't enough of him left to leave alive. They'd taken care to make sure no one would find his remains. Ever.

The new Colonel Anderson grinned into the mirror. "They did a better job on the teeth this time," he thought. "Last time the teeth almost blew my cover."

He glanced over at the briefcase on the seat next to him. The numbers on the dialing lock read: 0-1-3-6. That meant he had one hour and 36 minutes to complete his mission. Of course they hadn't given him the access code to reprogram the timer. But he wouldn't need it. He'd be out in plenty of time.

His superiors would be pleased that things were so far ahead of schedule. His country had been trying for decades to get someone on the inside, and he'd finally made it past the primary security checkpoint. Something no other agent had ever done.

With a grin on his face, he snuffed out his cigarette and reassured himself that his performance would probably mean a big increase in his paycheck. Maybe a couple extra zeros at the end of it. "Keep up the good work," he mumbled, "and you'll be impersonating a president someday."

He reached up and gently massaged the voice modulator that had been surgically installed in his throat. Kind of tough to get used to, but it was all part of the job.

He pulled into Colonel Anderson's parking space right next to building A-15, and headed inside.

"Well, here goes," he thought. "Let's see how well they disguised the bomb."

It took just over an hour to get past all the security checkpoints, metal detectors and searches. But no one even raised an eyebrow. Perfect. Everything was going according to plan.

Finally, he picked up his briefcase and headed for Corridor X. The most top secret wing of the base.

0-0-2-1

No one knew his real name or identity. Not even his own government. In his country, he was known only as "the Wolf." Wolves are great hunters. They rarely miss their targets. And they're masters at hiding in the shadows and delivering the lethal blow before their prey has any idea of their presence.

Exactly.

The Wolf stepped into room 33-B. "General, I came right away when you called."

"Good, Colonel," replied the general, lighting a cigarette. "Have a seat. Would you like a smoke?"

"No, sir. I don't smoke."

"Oh, yes. That's right. Nasty habit. . . . Well, then—" the general leaned over his desk as a red light flashed on the computer screen. "Just a moment, Colonel."

The Wolf sank into one of the leather-backed chairs and waited. *Sneak into the base undetected, plant the device and escape. That was his mission. He was so good he wasn't even sweating. Just another day at the office.*

The general glanced down at the computer screen on his desk and spoke into his headpiece microphone. "All right, Major, Yes. It's confirmed then? Alright. Send them in." Suddenly, he opened the desk drawer, pulled out his service revolver and aimed it at the Wolf's head. "It certainly was a good disguise," he said.

The Wolf blinked. "What are you talking about?"

"The disguise. Very well-done. Only a couple of groups in the world could have pulled it off. You passed voice recognition, retinal scans and even the instant fingerprint analysis on the doorknob to my office."

The Wolf just shook his head. "I don't know what you're talking about, General. It's me: Colonel Carter Anderson! We went to West Point together. Put the gun away and let's get on with business."

The general did not lower his gun.

"C'mon, we're both professionals, here. Cut the charade. What's your real name? Where is Colonel Anderson?"

The Wolf looked at the briefcase—0-0-1-2.

He paused to think. *Twelve minutes left. . . . Hm.*

Finally, he spoke in his natural Eastern European accent for the first time in six months. "Alright. How did you know?"

"The smell of smoke. I just had our guards check the ashtray of your car. You left a cigarette butt with your DNA on it. You can't fake DNA. Yours doesn't match the colonel's. There's always a clue. I've been in this business long enough to know that. There's always a clue. You can change how you look. But that doesn't make you a different person."

The Wolf knew when he was trapped. In one swift, smooth motion, he swung the briefcase up and knocked the end of the revolver from the general's hand. He leapt up and did a flying kick that caught the general in the forehead.

"There's no way out!" muttered the general from the floor.

"We'll see about that," laughed the Wolf.

But at that moment, six anti-terrorist military police burst through the door. In a matter of seconds they had the Wolf on the floor with his hands and feet secured.

The general stood up, brushing himself off. "Take him to Holding Cell 11."

"But sir, that's our only bomb-proof cell—"

"I know. Here, don't forget his briefcase. I have a feeling there's something in there you wouldn't want to take home to your family."

"But what do you want us to do with it?"

"Handcuff it to his wrist."

The Wolf's eyes grew large as he watched them handcuff the bomb to his left wrist.

0-0-0-7

"No, you don't understand!" yelled the Wolf. But they were already dragging him down the hallway to his cement-encased cell. And, as the door slammed shut in his face, he screamed "No!"

0-0-0-3

No one saw him furiously trying to reset the timer.

But, of course, it was too late.

0-0-0-0

CHECK IT OUT...

A wolf in sheep's clothing isn't easy to identify by its appearance, but you can always tell one by its actions. A hypocrite isn't known by his church attendance, but by his fruit or lifestyle. Just going to church has very little to do with being a follower of Jesus Christ.

Read what Jesus had to say about wolves in sheep's clothing in

Matthew 7:15-23. Notice in verses 21-23 that some wolves have even convinced themselves that they're sheep!

THINK IT OUT...

Christianity isn't only skin deep. It's not like a set of clothes you can put on and take off again. It's a once-and-for-all change from the inside out. It's more like a heart transplant than a skin graft. When you become a Christian, God doesn't just remodel your life. He rebuilds it from the ground up. He doesn't reshape your life. He gives you a whole new one.

So, those who have only an artificial, surface Christianity are really wolves in disguise.

LIVE IT OUT...

Are you more concerned with appearance than integrity? More worried about image than substance? Take a careful look at the type of fruit your life produces. Is it stuff like love, joy, peace, patience, kindness, goodness, faithfulness, gentleness and self-control (Galatians 5:22)—or nasty, rotten fruit that reveals your true self?

Don't mess with God. He wants you to be real. Even if you can pretend in front of others, God knows your heart. And the Good Shepherd can recognize a wolf a mile away.

PRAY IT OUT...

Spirit, you're the revealer of truth. Show me any areas of my life where I have only a skin-deep commitment. Change me from the inside out. I'm not gonna play games with you. Help me shed all the masks and all the disguises. See me for who I am, and help me to show that real self to others as well. Amen.

8

WINTERIZING YOUR CAR

It was spooky how much Bart and Alan had in common. Both were seniors, both went to the same high school, took the same classes, dated the same girls, got the same grades and lived on the same street in the same town in northern Minnesota. Land of 10,000 lakes, winter blizzards and hungry timber wolves.

And, both Bart and Alan wanted a car more than anything else for graduation.

For the last two years they'd both studied automobile maintenance in the tech classes at their school. They both knew cars inside and out. So, as graduation day neared, both Bart's dad and Alan's dad went car shopping. And finally, on graduation day, both guys received a gift from their dads.

Now, you gotta understand that neither of their families were all that well-off, so the cars weren't new or anything. But, you guessed it, both vehicles were the same make, model and year.

"Wow! This is awesome! Thanks, Dad!" said Bart.

"Wow! This is awesome! Thanks, Dad!" said Alan.

Both fathers cleared their throats. "Now, you'll need to take care of this car—"

"I know, I know. Check the air, change the oil, take it in for regular tuneups—" the boys said.

Both dads smiled, nodded and handed over the keys.

And that night, both Alan and Bart drove their cars to Swen's Pizzeria to celebrate. And when they got home, they both read through the owner's manual from cover to cover, taking notes.

Downright spooky.

Well, all summer long, Alan checked the air, changed the oil and took his car in for regular tuneups. But Bart didn't bother. "It's not the newest car," he reasoned. "Why waste all that time and energy maintaining it when it's headed for the junk heap anyway?"

Both cars ran well. Both cars were reliable. Both cars looked great.

And that autumn, both guys got jobs working at the same gas station at the other end of Wolf Lake.

Then, one day in October, Bart drove home and noticed Alan standing over the hood of his car.

"Car trouble?" he asked.

Alan nodded. "Just a little. I had to replace the belts and the air filter. Nothing serious. But I figured I'd winterize her while I was out here—break out the ice scraper, refill the wiper fluid, put on some snow tires. Stuff like that."

Bart smiled, "Sounds smart."

"Hey, I'm almost done. You need a hand getting your car ready for winter?"

"Naw, she's running like a dream. No problems at all. And besides, I'm kinda busy right now. I gotta work at the station tonight. Maybe next weekend."

Alan nodded. "Okay. See ya!"

The next weekend came and went. And the next. And the next. Bart's car still ran well. It was still reliable. It still looked great.

And each weekend, there was Alan out in the driveway, hard at work. Bart just shook his head. He didn't say anything, but he felt like telling his friend, "Look, if you wanna spend every free minute maintaining your car, have at it. I've got better things to do."

So, he didn't check the air pressure, change the oil or take his car in for a tuneup. And slowly, the tire pressure went down. Not much. Not so much that it was even noticeable. The oil became grungier and grungier. The rust spots on the bottom of the car got worse and worse. And the carburetor began to sputter.

But still, the car ran fine. So Bart didn't worry about it.

Then, one day, the snows came. A regular Minnesota-style blizzard. The heavy clouds dumped two feet of snow in less than a day. It's just the way things go in Minnesota. You know winter's coming, so you gotta be ready for it.

Bart was working at the gas station that day. "Big storm on the way," people said as they stopped in. "Break out the shovels! I hear they're closing the highway!" "Might be slippery driving home tonight."

And Bart nodded and smiled. He knew all that! After all, he'd lived in Minnesota his whole life! But he wasn't worried. "I can drive through this storm, no problemo," he thought.

Fewer and fewer people stopped by the station and finally, at 9:00 P.M. he locked it up and headed out into the storm.

It was slow going. There was zero visibility and the road was really icy. Halfway home, he ran out of windshield wiper fluid. He had to drive with his window open just to see outside. And then, as he was nearing the edge of Wolf Lake, he hit the patch of ice. Without snow tires, the car skidded sideways toward the snow bank.

Crunch.

As it hit the tree, the whole car just fell apart. All at once. The tires blew out. The engine dropped out of the rusty body of the car right onto the highway.

And great was the fall of it.

Problemo. Big problemo.

Bart stepped out of the car and looked around. He couldn't see anything but snow.

"Hm. This might not be good . . ." he thought. He went back and sat in the car to wait for help. But of course there were no other cars on the road that night. The highway patrol had indeed closed the highway. After all, only a fool would go out in a Minnesota blizzard in a junkie old car like that.

After about an hour, as the cold began to seep in, Bart heard the howls.

The wolves had found him.

And as for Alan? Well, his car lasted many, many years and he lived happily ever after.

It was amazing how little they had in common. Downright amazing.

CHECK IT OUT...

Jesus did not use the story of the wise and foolish builders to point out the difference between knowing him and not knowing him. Carefully read his story in Matthew 7:21-29. What *was* he contrasting?

THINK IT OUT...

See the context? Jesus said that not everyone who claims to know him actually does (verses 21-23). And since that's the case, those who put his words into practice are wise because their futures are secure. But those who don't put them into practice are foolish and will have nothing to show for it in the end.

The only difference between the two people in Jesus' story was that the wise man put God's Word *into practice* and the fool didn't. That's it. That's the difference. Both heard his words. Both knew them. But only one obeyed.

The rock-solid foundation is obedience to Jesus' words.

Knowing right from wrong isn't what counts. Applying truth is what matters. Making a difference for Christ means building your life on his teachings by *putting them into practice* in every area of your life.

LIVE IT OUT...

Over time, a life that isn't lived for God will fall apart. It'll rust out and collapse under the weight of everyday pressures. It'll crumble when you least expect it—and you'll be crushed when it does. It may look good on the outside, and even run well for awhile. But it's gonna break down. It's just a matter of time.

Are you regularly putting God's Word into practice? Are you finding practical ways to follow Jesus in thought, word and deed? If not, you're more like the idiot who built his house on quicksand than the wise guy who laid a concrete foundation.

PRAY IT OUT...

Jesus, most of the time I really do know what I should do. I just don't always do it. Forgive me for that. I don't wanna end up like the foolish guy. I wanna be like the wise builder who built on a solid foundation by living his life for you. Choice by choice, day by day. The storms are gonna come. That's for certain. And the only way to be prepared is to build my life moment by moment on you and your Word. Help me do it starting right now. Amen.

9

TROUBLE AT THE CONCESSION STAND

"Can you believe this new guy?" Antoine asked his friend Trevor as they arrived at their hall lockers one Friday after school. "What a wannabe!"

"Yeah, no kidding," said Trevor opening his locker and pulling out his letter jacket. "What's the deal with him, anyway? He doesn't even own a letter jacket and he calls himself a basketball player. What's with that? And he doesn't even have the right kind of shoes! He just wears old worn-out sneakers."

"Worn-out sneakers! How can you play basketball with old shoes?"

"Well the simple answer is you can't. But that's just the tip of the iceberg," replied Trevor, slipping on his letter jacket and straightening it so that anyone who passed by could see his name and all his medals. "I saw him playing the other day, and his socks didn't match."

"What!" Antoine said horrified. "You mean one was pulled up higher than the other?"

"Yup."

"Whoa."

Antoine and Trevor grabbed their leather basketballs from their lockers and headed down the hall toward the gym to make sure the concession stand was well-stocked for that night's game against St. Mary's High School.

When they reached the stairs that led down to the locker room, Antoine broke the silence, "You know what I heard? I heard he doesn't even shoot with both feet on the ground. He jumps up into the air to shoot. Whoever heard of leaving the ground? It's gotta be against the rules somewhere. People have been shooting with both feet on the ground ever since the game was invented. How disrespectful to the great St. Naismith, rest his soul, to shoot like that."

At the mention of St. Naismith, they both very reverently made the sign of the peach basket in the air in front of them.

"Who does he think he is, shooting in the air?" said Trevor. "I'll bet he can't even spin a ball on his finger!"

Antoine nodded his head in agreement, "Yeah. Anyone who can't do that doesn't even deserve to check into the game."

By now they were at the bottom of the stairs. Each of them still carried his ball. They never actually played with these basketballs, of course. They were much too expensive for that. Instead, they just carried them back and forth between their lockers so people would be sure to notice that they were members of the basketball team.

"This new guy doesn't even look like a basketball player to me," said Trevor, opening the locker-room door. "I'll bet his dad wasn't even a coach!"

"Nobody really knows for sure who his dad is," Antoine whispered. "I've heard some people say he's . . . a janitor."

"A janitor!" gasped Trevor. "From where?"

"Idaho."

"Idaho! How could any good players come from Idaho? They don't even have a professional team there!" Trevor said, leading the way through the maze of lockers toward the showers where the lockers of honor were located.

"This new guy is obviously a loser. Lenny told me a couple other things you won't believe. He said this new guy dribbles with either hand, not just his right hand. And he can't even sing a note. How is he supposed to sing the national anthem before the games? I also heard—and you're not gonna believe this—he doesn't watch college basketball on TV on Saturday. Instead he volunteers at the YMCA teaching little kids how to shoot free throws. Do you believe it?"

"I don't believe it."

"I knew you wouldn't," responded Antoine, satisfied. Both of them changed into their game uniforms, laced up their $400 basketball shoes and headed toward the gym.

As Trevor opened the gym doors, he heard the sound of a basketball bouncing on the floor. Sure enough, it was the new guy, practicing. Again.

"Hey, what are you doing in here?" Trevor yelled across the gym floor. "That's where the concession stand is supposed to be! Where are all the tables and boxes of candy?!"

"This is a gymnasium, not a grocery store!" the new guy shouted, obviously annoyed. "I cleared that stuff outta here so we could get serious about the game! A gym is for hoops! Not popcorn and bubble gum!"

Antoine and Trevor were furious! They'd spent hours the night before stacking up those boxes of candy in the corner of the gym. The pep club made a nice little profit selling snacks during the home games.

"How dare you lecture us about basketball!" Antoine yelled back. "We don't even know who you are or where you're from! Look at the way you shoot! It's obvious you've never been coached. Where did you get permission to practice in our gym, anyway?"

"My dad gave me the keys!"

"Your dad, huh!" said Trevor. "Well, our dads are coaches! What does your dad do? Sweep the gym!?"

The new guy turned and faced them. "My dad is a ballplayer and he taught me everything I know! Look at you two. You're out-of-shape, you never work out—you spend more time in front of the mirror than on the court! You're more concerned with how you look during the pregame warm-ups than how you perform in the games! And all you do is complain about anyone who doesn't play zone defense!"

"Zone defense is what our fathers taught us to play! It's what they played, and their fathers played and their fathers played, all the way back to St. Naismith, rest his soul." At the mention of his name, both Trevor and Antoine very reverently made the sign of the peach basket.

But the new guy didn't. He just shook his head. "You two look like players. You dress like players. You even act like ballplayers, but inside you guys are only a couple of cheerleaders for yourselves!"

When he finished speaking, the new guy turned around, jumped into the air and swished a thirty-footer.

Trevor and Antoine were so mad they didn't know what to say.

"Wait 'til tonight!" Trevor blurted out. "Just wait 'til tonight!"

But that night, as the crowd cheered, the new guy poured in 30 points and snagged 15 rebounds. There was a big article in the newspaper about him. Trevor and Antoine weren't even mentioned.

That did it. They'd had it. From that day on, Trevor and Antoine began plotting ways to get the new guy cut from the team. They spread rumors, got some people to claim they'd seen him cheating in English Lit., and finally, he was suspended indefinitely from school.

But he didn't disappear forever. Stories surfaced that he was still showing up at the YMCA and at playgrounds around town. But Trevor and Antoine refused to believe it. They figured he'd moved back to Idaho to farm potatoes or something. He wasn't their problem anymore.

But that's when things began to change.

Players all around the league began dribbling with either hand and swishing 30-foot jumpers. And, strangest of all, a few players began taking off at the free-throw line, floating through the air and slam-dunking over their opponents. Almost like the law of gravity didn't apply to them.

Yeah, he'd changed the way the game is played, alright. And basketball would never be the same again.

CHECK IT OUT...

Jesus' archenemies were the leaders in the church. They just couldn't accept the idea that he was really God suited up as a human being. You can get a feel for how he felt about them by reading Matthew 21:12, 13 and Matthew 23:23-36.

THINK IT OUT...

Jesus didn't fit in very well with the religious people of his day. They never accused him of being too holy. Instead, they called him (among other things) a blasphemous, gluttonous, illegitimate, insane, demon-possessed, inebriated half-breed.

Jesus had names for them as well. He called them a bunch of whiny, hypocritical little brats. He said they were like zombies in tuxedoes—dressed up nice and neat, but filled with maggots and filth. And he called them morons, snakes, sons of Hell and spiritually blind children of the devil. Yikes.

LIVE IT OUT...

Many people today are more concerned about what people think of them than what God thinks of them. They'd rather cover up the smell by adding a few more layers of deodorant than just take a shower and get clean.

What about you? Are you more worried about your clothes than your heart? Are you looking for an audience with people rather than intimacy with God? Are you quick to pile up rule after rule for others, and then quick to find loopholes for yourself? If that's you, guess what? You have a lot more in common with Jesus' archenemies than with him.

PRAY IT OUT...

God, I don't wanna act. I wanna be. I don't wanna play the part. I wanna live it. Jesus, I know that religious rituals can never make me a new person, only you can. Today I come before you and ask that you make me new. I wanna play on your team. Amen.

10

WANNA KNOW WHAT I DID LAST NIGHT?

As I lie in bed, even before I open my eyes, I know things will never be the same again. Not after last night. It's weird how quickly things can change.

I mean, it's not like I wanted to do it. I really didn't. I was just there at the wrong place at the wrong time and before I knew what was happening, I'd said "yes" to some things that didn't seem all that bad at the time. Now they do. And everything is different. Everything.

I can hear Mom calling that it's time to get up and go to school. So I slide out of bed and escape into the bathroom before my older sister Kim can see me.

Oh, my God, what have I done! I wish I could change it all, go back and undo what happened last night!

But I can't. What's done is done.

I feel like crying, but don't. So I begin to turn away from the mirror, when I notice my eyes. They look so sad. And afraid.

Maybe if I pretend hard enough, act happy enough, no one will notice how different I am.

So I try out different faces, like an actress practicing for an audition and then all of a sudden I hear Kim pounding on the door.

"Audrey! Are you in there? Hurry up! I gotta take a shower before school!"

I don't say anything and she yells at me again, "Audrey!" I see the doorknob twisting violently back and forth.

"I'm hurrying, I'm hurrying!" I shout, still looking in the mirror, trying on another smile.

I can do it. I can fool them. Maybe they'll never find out.

How did I get myself into this? I'm scared I won't be able to hide and at the same time afraid I will. If they find out, they'll hate me, but if they don't find out, I'll always have to live with this guilt—

"Audrey!"

I unlock the door, yank it open and push past Kim without even looking at her. I grab my stuff and I walk downstairs. And there stands Mom.

"Good morning, Audrey. How are you?"

I pretend to smile. "Great, Mom."

She looks at me and for a second it seems like she can tell. I turn away. There's a part of me that wants her to know. But I can't tell her. If I keep pretending, maybe it'll all work out. In time, maybe even I can forget about it.

So, I go to school and keep on smiling. But there's a thousand little things that remind me of what I've done. I see a chalkboard and all I can think of is God standing there in Heaven, writing down all the evil things I've done with a big circle around last night. That scares me. I want things to get back to normal. But I know they won't. It's too late.

What frightens me the most is that maybe, just maybe, I've finally gone too far. Maybe God won't want me anymore. If you knew what I did last night, you'd be afraid too.

No, please don't let this be happening! I was only curious! I didn't mean to do it!

In the library I'm supposed to be downloading this stuff for my English paper when I accidentally double-click on "delete" rather than "move text." So I'm freaked I can't get the information back and I run to the librarian.

But he shakes his head. "I'm sorry. With this software, once you've erased it from the computer's memory it's permanent. You can't retrieve that information again. It's gone forever."

Great. Just great. Gone forever, just like my old life.

So a week goes by and I keep on pretending. Then another week. And another. And I'm still pretending, but the guilt is still there. I stop looking in mirrors because they make me remember. I can tell I'm treating people differently, and I get angry easier, even when I'm not really angry at them. I still feel dirty after I take a shower. And then Kim comes up to me one night after supper. And she gets really serious and says, "Can I talk to you?"

And I don't think it's anything big so I say, "Sure, what's up?"

Then she sits down next to me on the couch and whispers, "I've been hearing some stuff at school."

My hands start getting sweaty. "What kind of stuff?"

She looks down at the floor and then back up at me. "You've been acting different. . . . I heard . . ."

"What did you hear?" I'm breathing faster now. My heart is hammering.

"I heard you've been doing drugs."

The words slam into my gut like a sledgehammer. I can feel myself get angry and scared and accused and defensive all at once. "What? From who?" The words come stumbling out.

"It doesn't matter. Is it true?"

I don't know what to say, but something inside of me erupts and I start crying. I can't seem to help it. I don't want her to see me like this, but I can't stop.

"It isn't drugs," I whisper.

Now, she's got her arm around me and she's hugging me. And even though I'm embarrassed to do it, I lean my head into her shoulder.

"Then what is it?" she asks.

"I can't say," I mumble. "I'm scared. I'm too scared."

"Did you . . . break the law or something?" I hear a hint of worry in her voice.

"I . . . I . . . I broke God's law, I guess." I don't know any other way to say it.

There's a long pause. I figure she's searching for what to say next. Finally she says, "Have you told him about it?"

"Who?"

"God."

"God? He already knows . . ." I said, wishing he didn't.

Now she's up, getting me some tissues from the kitchen. "Did you ask him to forgive you?"

I want to scream, not to her but to the world, *"Of course! I've been begging him to forgive me ever since it happened!"* But I only mutter, "Yeah."

"Then he doesn't know."

"He doesn't know what?"

"What you did." She sits back down next to me.

I turn to look at her. "What are you talking about?"

"Listen. If you've admitted it and asked him to forgive you, he has. And when he forgives, he forgets. It doesn't matter how many times you've done it, or how horrible it was."

"But you don't know what I did! There's no excuse!"

"I've done bad stuff, too, Audrey. Stuff I've never told you or anyone else about. But I know he's forgiven me. It doesn't matter how bad it was or how big it was. God's love is bigger."

God's love is bigger?

It takes a few minutes for her words to sink in. I wonder for a moment about the things she's done but never told me about. . . .

Could it be. . . . Had she done it, too?

Finally, I tell her thanks and wipe my eyes and walk upstairs by myself. But inside I feel pretty much the same.

So there I am surfing the Net trying to forget about everything and sort it all out and for some reason I remember that day in the library when my stuff got deleted. *Once it's erased . . . it's permanent . . . gone forever.*

Hm.

Then the next day at school, I'm sitting there looking at the chalkboard thinking of God again, when all of a sudden I notice the eraser. And Kim's words come back to me: *When he forgives, he forgets. . . . God's love is bigger. . . .*

Is it true? Is his forgiveness that great? His love that deep? I've never needed that much love before. Could he really forgive *and forget?*

As I'm staring at the board, I start thinking, *God isn't sitting up in Heaven with a piece of chalk keeping track of all my sins. He's got an eraser instead. And that eraser is wide enough to wipe away the guilt of what I did that night. Delete it forever.*

All of a sudden, for the first time since it happened, I'm not scared. It's like a part of me is set free.

I can hardly wait for the bell. As soon as it rings, I run to the bathroom and stare into the mirror. My eyes! It's me again! No pretending!

It's about a week later when I walk by Kim's room and she calls to me.

"Hey, Audrey! C'mere a sec."

"Yeah?"

"You look a lot better."

"Thanks. I feel better."

She pauses, but I can tell she's not done. She wants to ask me something. Finally, she just sorta blurts it out. "By the way, I've been wondering. What was it you did, anyway?"

"You really want to know?" I ask, leaning against the side of her door.

She doesn't answer, but I know that's a "Yes!"

"The same thing you did," I say.

She's got this disappointed gimme-a-break-I'm-your-big-sister look on her face. "But you don't know what I've done," she says.

"That's right," I answer. "I have no idea what you've done."

And I'm smiling as I head to my room. I figure maybe I'll spend the afternoon deleting some old files from the computer. After all, they're just taking up space, anyway.

CHECK IT OUT...

It's pretty surprising to learn that Jesus talked a lot more about how we should forgive other people than about how God forgives us. In Luke 17:3-5, he says we should confront sin in the lives of others, but then be willing to forgive them when they repent. Even if they turn right around and hurt us again.

THINK IT OUT...

How often do you forgive yourself when you mess up? What about others? Is it harder to forgive them than yourself? God forgives and forgets, and Jesus wants us to do the same.

How many times should we forgive? Over and over and over and over, Jesus said, because that's how you act and God still forgives you. Don't ignore sin, confront it. Like Kim did. She cared enough to talk with her sister. Don't hold grudges or give guilt trips—forgive. And then forget. Just like God.

LIVE IT OUT...

God really does forgive and forget (see Jeremiah 31:34). Are there things you've done and can't seem to forget, even though God has? You don't need to carry the guilt or shame around any longer. Jesus already did. He carried your sin all the way to the cross to provide a real solution to our sin problem. Turn to him. Talk to him about it today. Let his love set you free.

PRAY IT OUT...

God, just like Audrey, I have things in my life that I wonder about. Bad things I've done that no one else knows about. In faith I come to you today and ask you to forgive me and help me forgive others. Wipe the slate clean and give me the joy that comes from knowing true and lasting forgiveness. I'm all yours, God. No more pretending. Amen.

11

CREATURES OF THE NIGHT

Jessie yawned as she walked over to the window and closed the curtains to shut out the night. Outside, the night air was starting to get cool as autumn crept into the city once again. A persistent wind had been blowing wild gray clouds over the streets all day. She could feel the breeze slicing through a long narrow crack in the plaster. "I'll have to fix that crack one of these days," she said to herself. "It feels like winter is almost here." She shivered slightly, turned and walked upstairs to the bathroom.

Ever since the day she saw the rat, darkness had made her uneasy.

No one knew for sure what had first attracted it. Maybe it was the crumbs on the counter by the sink. Or the old boxes of cereal in the cupboard. Maybe the rat was just trying to find a warm place to spend the winter. Or maybe—as the guy from the animal control center had said nonchalantly—it was rabid and that's why it hadn't been afraid to come inside.

"Rabid?" she'd said.

"Yes, ma'am. Means it's got rabies—a viral disease that affects mammals. Messes up their central nervous system. Nearly always drives 'em crazy. They lose their fear of people. It's transmitted through their bite. It's fatal—"

"What!?" she gasped.

"Afraid so, ma'am. Very deadly. Put out some traps and rat poison and make sure those cracks in the plaster are sealed up before winter comes. If there's a way into this house, they'll find it."

At first she'd been very careful. The whole rat thing really shook her up. So, she did as he said. She cleaned the whole house. She started doing the dishes every night and she was careful not to leave any open food in the pantry. She bought a couple of traps and checked them daily. She even thought about getting a cat.

But then, once the house was clean and there were no more rat droppings around, she thought, *I don't want to overreact. I mean, the rat is gone. I haven't seen any sign of it for weeks. Let's not get carried away, here! I don't want rat poison sitting out in my house! I'm sure I'll be fine if I just keep things cleaned up a little. I don't really need a cat and those cracks in the wall aren't big enough to let a rat through. It must have just snuck in when I left the garage door open one night.*

So, eventually she threw away the rat traps and prided herself on how nice and clean she was able to keep her house.

Jessie brushed her teeth and then poured herself a glass of water. Outside, the wind scratched some tree limbs across the bathroom window startling her so that she nearly dropped her water onto the floor. "Settle down, Jess!" she said aloud. "It's alright! The house is clean now. No more rats."

She walked into the bedroom and sighed. *I'm probably just tired,* she thought. And it was true. She was exhausted. It had been an incredibly long week at work. *But tonight I'm gonna sleep like a log.*

Jessie changed into her nightgown, climbed under the covers and flicked off the light. She didn't notice the small set of eyes blinking at her from the corner of the room.

As she closed her eyes and told herself there was nothing to worry about, one dark form after another eased out of the crack in the wall and scurried over to the bed. And they weren't looking for cereal or bread crumbs. These rats were hungry for meat. So, one by one, they crawled up the bedposts toward the figure snoring softly on the mattress.

And then, as her breathing became steady and the deep sleep she'd been yearning for took over, they slipped noiselessly beneath the covers, surrounded their meal and began to chew.

CHECK IT OUT...

Jesus told the bizarre, unsettling story about "The Demons Who Came Back" in Luke 11:23-26. It's a pretty creepy, nightmarish tale. Notice that the person in his story was worse off at the end, *after* cleaning up his life.

THINK IT OUT...

Demons have one goal—destroying humans for eternity. They are evil. They are persistent. And they are real.

Now, think about Jesus' story. It starts right after the exorcism. A demon has just been driven out of someone's life. That person starts living a good, clean life. But he takes no precautions to make sure the demons can't get back in. And then, after awhile, a whole horde of demons returns to invade his life again. Permanently.

Jesus said we're either for him or against him. There's no middle ground. You gotta stand on one side or the other. You're either in his camp or you're in enemy territory. Someone's gonna be first in your life. And it's either gonna be Jesus or . . . well, you get the picture.

LIVE IT OUT...

Just cleaning up your life isn't enough. Just being good isn't good enough. What cracks have you left unattended? How does sin slip in undetected in your life? Have you been tidying up your life without inviting Christ in to stay? If you try to get rid of sin without inviting him in, it'll return stronger than ever.

Your soul must serve someone. Your heart must have a master. Who will it be?

PRAY IT OUT...

Lord, sometimes I get comfortable and complacent thinking I can just tidy up my life without you. But that's a lie. So, take over. Fill me, Holy Spirit. Come on into the deepest recesses of my life. From the farthest corners of my imagination to the innermost reaches of my mind, patch up the cracks where evil thoughts like to seep in. I don't wanna be clean and vulnerable, I wanna be filled with you. Amen.

12

NO ONE WILL EVER KNOW...

Jordan and Wesley left the video store and drove up Legion Hill, where all the doctors and lawyers lived. "You never told me it was up here!" said Wesley.

"Yeah, wait till you see it," said Jordan. "Um, take a left here and then a right. . . . It's the first house on the right."

Wesley turned the car up a long driveway that led to the mansion.

"Whoa! Check this place out! Man, you scored big time!"

Jordan just smiled. It really was a sweet deal. One of his professors was working on a book in Scotland and was letting Jordan stay in the house all summer—rent-free.

Yeah, he had a few jobs to do—mow the lawn, water the plants, pick up the mail and stuff like that. But it was definitely worth it.

"Yeah, it's pretty awesome," said Jordan. "Let me show you around the estate."

He took Wesley on a tour of the garden, the pool, the game room. Everything.

"So you just hang out here all summer! Man, I can't *believe* you!"

"Pretty sweet, huh?"

Wesley just shook his head. Suddenly, his eyes lit up. "Hey! I've got an awesome idea!"

"What's that?"

"Let's throw a party! We'll get some kegs, invite some friends—I mean it's all here! Swimming pool, whirlpool, sauna . . ."

Jordan walked over to the fridge to grab a soda. "I can't do that, man. I made a deal that I wouldn't let anyone in here. If a lot of people came over and word leaked out . . . well, let's just say it wouldn't be good."

"Why not?" asked Wesley. "What's the worst that could happen?"

"I could lose my scholarship—Professor Willis is on my advisory committee. I'd lose my graduate assistantship for sure, and this is my senior year! No, I'd better not chance it. C'mon, let's just watch the movie."

Wesley shrugged his shoulders. "Okay, whatever."

But he didn't give up. As the summer wore on, Wesley kept bringing up the whole party thing and Jordan kept telling him to forget about it.

"No one will ever know, trust me!" said Wesley.

But Jordan would shake his head. "You're not listening. This place isn't mine! I'm just taking care of it until my professor gets back."

But then summer passed and school began. And Jordan's professor didn't return.

"Don't you ever hear anything?" asked Wesley.

"I used to," said Jordan. "I got e-mails all the time at the beginning of the summer. I wonder what happened."

September came and went. Still no word.

"You think maybe Dr. Willis died or something?" asked Wesley. "I mean, why else would anyone take this long?"

Jordan just shook his head. "I really don't know."

And that's when he started seriously thinking about holding a party.

Something terrible must have happened or else Dr. Willis would have been back by now. The school year was in full swing! *I don't suppose Professor Willis is ever coming back!* thought Jordan. *And if that's the case, there's no sense letting this place go to waste! Why* shouldn't *I have a party?*

So, the first weekend of October he went up to Wesley. "Okay, man. Invite your friends. We're gonna have a party. But you gotta promise me they're not gonna get too wild! And no minors, okay?"

Wesley smiled. "No problem. Trust me. It'll be great!"

So that night, Wesley's friends came over. About 20 people in all. And they behaved themselves. They didn't stay too late. They didn't trash the house. No one got drunk.

And the next day Jordan surveyed the house. Nothing was broken. Just a few bottles left laying around by the pool. *Hm,* he thought. *That wasn't so bad. And it didn't hurt anything. It was fun! Maybe we could have a few more people over next weekend.*

From then on, they partied every weekend. And, for the most part, people behaved themselves. But each party got a little bigger and a little wilder.

Fall slipped past. Winter came and went. Spring arrived. Still no professor. Still no word. Just more and more parties.

One day, Jordan grinned. "Let's pull out all the stops this Friday! We'll order a few dozen pizzas and have 50 kegs of beer!"

"But how are we gonna pay for all that?" asked Wesley.

"I found a few of my professor's credit cards lying around. We'll just use those!"

So they did.

And that night, more than 200 students came over. And it didn't take long at all for things to spill out of control. They made designs by pouring beer onto the lush carpet. They busted windows, broke up the furniture and drove their cars through the garden. The more drunk the people got, the less they wore into the swimming pool. And they took turns pairing off and disappearing into the master bedroom.

Finally, in the middle of the night, one last car arrived. A woman stepped out and looked around at the students passed out on the lawn. She looked a little old to be coming to a frat party, but she walked up to the door anyhow and let herself in.

A few people offered her a beer as she walked past the swimming pool. She declined.

She looked around carefully and eventually made her way upstairs to the master bedroom. When she knocked, no one answered.

The woman tried the door. It was locked. But that didn't matter. She had the key.

She unlocked it and pulled open the door.

And there was Jordan, drunk and half-naked. In bed with a girl. They were both passed out.

She could have lost control. Finding your house in that condition would be enough to push most people over the edge. But she just walked over to the phone and quietly called the police.

They took Jordan away that night. And the drinking charges were the least of his worries. Credit card fraud. Vandalism. And the girl he'd been with was underage. They read him his rights and explained that having sex with a minor constituted statutory rape. Ten to twenty years, they said. Plus all the fines for the damage on the house.

But he just snickered and shouted, "What a party!" He was too drunk to realize how busted he was.

And before going to bed, Professor Willis ripped up Jordan's scholarship papers. Sure, she felt a little sad about the house, but she felt worse about her student. She'd really liked him. It was a shame to lose a good student like that. Especially so close to graduation.

"Oh, well," she said. "He made his choice."

And then she went to bed and she didn't lose any sleep over Jordan.

Not even a wink.

CHECK IT OUT...

Whoa. Imagine getting caught like that and losing everything in one terrible moment. It's gonna happen to some people. Jesus predicted it would. Check it out for yourself in Luke 12:39-48.

THINK IT OUT...

Was Jesus out to scare people? If not, why would he include such a violent and brutal ending (verses 46, 47)? Why do people think God won't find out about their choices? Do you ever think like that? What does this story tell you about God's attitude toward those who don't take him seriously?

LIVE IT OUT...

The student became careless and irresponsible. He took advantage of his professor's trust, and then he lost everything. Jesus said those who've been entrusted with much are responsible for much. Have you been entrusted with much? Compared to whom? What are you doing with it?

Remain watchful; be responsible with what God has entrusted to you. The master will return after (not before) you expect him. Live today as if you expected Jesus to return at any moment.

PRAY IT OUT...

Dear God, sometimes I look for loopholes. I want to find safe ways to sin. When no one is looking. When I don't think I'll get caught. When it doesn't look like it'll hurt anyone else. But the truth is that you're always nearby, watching me and that one day soon you're gonna come back. Keep me watchful, awake and faithful. Especially when it seems like no one else will ever know. Amen.

13

CONFESSIONS OF A SECRET ADMIRER

He watches her talking on the phone, giggling, and he remembers how things used to be. Back when they were together, when he would hold her head against his shoulder, wipe the tears off her cheek, wrap his arms around her . . .

It all seems so long ago.

But she has new friends now. And she's so busy with her job at the water park, going to the beach, hanging out at the mall . . . And whenever she sees him, she looks away. She must be trying to forget.

How long has it been? It wasn't his idea to break up; she just seemed to lose interest in him. First she started avoiding him on the weekends, then she stopped meeting him for lunch. She never even said good-bye, just sorta drifted away one choice at a time. Wandering off to another's arms. . . .

● ●

"Hey, Lindsey, your parents home?"

"Not tonight, Bryan. Why, what did you have in mind?" Absently, she twirled the phone cord around her finger. Her heart was racing.

"How 'bout I come over for awhile and, you know, we watch TV or something?"

She paused for a moment before answering. She heard the hint in his voice. She knew what he was thinking. More than once Bryan had lain next to her to watch a movie and slid his hand up her shirt as they lost interest in the show. She knew it was wrong, but finally, she said, "Okay, see you in about an hour?"

"I'll be there."

As she hung up the phone, she smiled.

Lindsey Rayman was on top of the world. She had a great job and cool friends, school had just let out, and she was free for the summer. Best of all, she was going out with Bryan, the cutest guy in her class.

Yeah, things were good. . . . All except for the voice.

Every once in a while, in the back of her mind she could hear it whispering, *Remember me, Lindsey? Remember how things used to be? Wanna get back together?*

She kinda felt guilty. After all, they really had been close. And they'd shared so much.

But what was the big deal, anyway? I mean, she still talked to him; she didn't ignore him completely. Yeah, it was small talk, never anything really deep or important and she didn't tell him her secrets anymore, but what can you expect? She had a life to live!

After all, she knew Bryan wouldn't approve of them spending time together. She knew the types of things Bryan was into, the stuff he did, the little comments he made. The last thing she wanted was for Bryan to find out about their relationship.

And besides, he was so different from Bryan. She didn't feel like explaining herself to him or defending the things she'd been doing since they broke up. . . .

So, she'd made a few mistakes, so what? The stuff she and Bryan did wasn't half as bad as what most of her friends were doing.

And it was worth it. I mean, she was popular these days. Things were finally coming together.

Lindsey turned away from the phone and headed upstairs to change clothes and straighten up her room. She propped some pillows on the bed and turned the TV to face it. As she passed the mirror, she glanced at her reflection. "I'm just the same old Lindsey," she told herself; "I haven't changed." But in her heart she knew something was definitely different. The more excuses she made, the busier she became—the more she tried to ignore the voice—the emptier she felt.

● ●

From where he is standing, he watches her clean her room and knows it's because Bryan is coming over. He sees her stare into the mirror again. And he knows why—she's trying to see if the real Lindsey is still there. She's trying to convince herself that everything is okay, that she doesn't need him.

It's times like these that hurt the most.

But he loves her anyway. He'll always love her. And he'll keep waiting for her. He'd do anything for her.

She's worth it.

• •

As she cleared off her desk, she noticed the collection of love letters.

He'd written her dozens of letters and stories and poems. All bound together in a little book.

"Oh no!" she thought. "What if Bryan sees this? I can't just leave it lying around!"

Suddenly, the doorbell rang.

She grabbed the book and lifted it toward the shelf, but in her haste a page flipped open and she saw the words he'd written to her so long ago.

And like water bursting through a dam, she began to remember. The long walks, the late nights, the times he was there for her when no one else was, the way he gave her strength when she felt helpless, how he filled her with hope when she had nowhere to turn. She remembered the rejection and ridicule he put up with—all for her. And that promise he'd made, *"I'll always be here for you, Lindsey. I've loved you with an everlasting love. Nothing could ever make me stop loving you."*

How long had it been now?

She used to tell everyone the best day of her life was when they first met. . . .

The doorbell rang again.

Oh no, what had she done? All those times she'd been silent while her friends made fun of him . . . Those things she'd laughed at . . . The excuses she'd made . . . Those nights with Bryan! How could this have happened? Could he ever forgive her? Would he want her back after the way she'd treated him?

"Hey, Lindsey! You up there? What's going on?" Bryan eased open the front door. "Lindsey?"

She used to read and reread these pages every day! How had her love grown so cold? Being popular wasn't worth it if she couldn't have him. . . .

She folded her Bible shut. "I'm sorry," she whispered, closing her eyes. "I'm so sorry. . . ."

Bryan called up to her once more before cussing and walking away. But Lindsey didn't hear him, she was pouring her heart out to the one she'd left behind, the one who'd been waiting for her.

And as she prayed, her secret admirer wrapped his arms around her again, just like he used to. *"Of course I forgive you, Lindsey. I told you I'd be here for you no matter what. I love you. I'll always love you."*

"I'm glad you're back, Jesus," she thought.

But then she heard the voice again, *"Lindsey, I never left. You did. . . . But all that's over now. We're finally back together. No more tears, now. It's time to celebrate!"*

And as she sat listening, she knew there was one thing left to do. Tomorrow she would call Bryan and introduce him to her secret admirer.

After all, it was about time they met.

CHECK IT OUT...

In Luke 15, Jesus told three stories about lost items. Read the first two stories in verses 1-10. How are they similar? How are they different?

God's method is to seek, find and celebrate. See how Jesus emphasized the same pattern in each of his stories? Jesus even said that his entire mission on earth was to "seek and to save what was lost" (Luke 19:10).

THINK IT OUT...

Have you ever had a pet who ran away? If so, did you look for your lost pet? How hard did you search? Why? Think of a time you were lost. What lured you away? How did you know when you were found?

The point of Jesus' stories isn't so much that we're lost. Or even that he searches for us. Rather, his emphasis is on the joyful celebration upon our return. God takes partying seriously. Jesus attended so many parties with the wrong kind of people, the church leaders called him a glutton and drunk! And that didn't bug him at all because his favorite description of what Heaven is—you guessed it—a party.

LIVE IT OUT...

They gasped because he welcomed and ate with sinners. His response? He had to celebrate! Because he'd finally found them! And therefore, they'd found him.

But those who refuse to be found are gonna miss out on the party.

What brought Lindsey back? Whose voice was whispering to her heart? How do you know that? (See John 10:27, 28.)

Like Lindsey, it's easy to get distracted and lose sight of our first love. It's easy to let artificial sweeteners replace the real thing. Don't settle for second best. If you've wandered, Jesus wants you back. Listen to his voice and let him lead you home.

PRAY IT OUT...

God, just like that sheep, I need to be found. I've wandered. My thoughts. My words. My life. I've left the fold more than once. Carry me back! Bring me home! Wrap your arms around me and let me know your presence. Speak to me from the Bible, your Word. And then, Lord, help me reach out to other lost souls who need to find their way home, too. Amen.

14

ALONE ON THE PORCH

"Oh great! Just great!" yelled Jerod Westenberg as he watched his dad walk back toward the house. "Leave me here to think it over, huh?! Well, I've already thought it over! Don't walk away from me! Do you hear me! I've made my decision. I'm gonna stay right here! DO YOU HEAR ME?!"

He watched his father disappear inside, closing the sliding patio door partway to keep out the chilly autumn air. The door stood half open.

Jerod slumped onto the deck chair next to the pool and waited. Dad would be back. He knew that. Dad would come back outside and beg him—Jerod Westenberg—to come in. Or maybe he'd feel bad and move the party outside to include him. That's the kind of softhearted guy Dad was. "So, all I gotta do is wait it out. I can outlast the old man," he reasoned. "It's just a matter of time."

He turned and glanced toward the door. He could see through the glass into the kitchen. People were getting sodas and passing around bowls of chips and nachos. A couple of pizzas lay on the counter. He could smell them from where he sat. As he stared at the house, someone turned on some music. The party was getting into full swing. Jerod shook his head as he remembered his father's words. . . . *"Are you kidding me? We gotta celebrate! Your brother is back! C'mon in, join the party!"*

He had to celebrate, huh? He had to throw a party?! A party for a loser like Ted! *Has he ever thrown a party for me?* thought Jerod. *Has he ever told me to invite a few friends over for a barbeque? Or to watch videos and play a little Twister? I don't think so.*

Jerod got up and began to pace back and forth beside the pool. "So that's how it's gonna be," he said to himself. "I put in all those late nights. I sacrifice my own dreams to make the family business work. I go to college to get a business degree so we can keep up with the changing landscape of today's global markets. And this is the thanks I get?!"

He turned and kicked over one of those deck tables with the green and white umbrellas sticking out of the middle. It fell into the pool and slowly sank to the bottom.

From inside the house, rock music drifted out the open door. It almost sounded like they'd turned up the stereo. Unbelievable. How dare they? How dare they celebrate? It was like they were mocking him. It made him want to throw up.

Jerod had always followed the rules. He never got into trouble. He'd held onto a good job all through college and still managed to keep his grades up. He'd even taken time off from his graduate work back when Dad was sick. Sure, Dad would tell him to take a break sometimes, that he didn't have to put in all those extra hours, that he could take some time off and enjoy himself. Maybe go golfing a little. Or spend the weekend fishing.

But Jerod knew how things worked in the world. If you wanna get ahead, you gotta outwork the competition. Oh, yeah. Jerod knew. "I can earn his love. If I just work hard enough he'll be obligated to give me the family business when he retires. He'll owe it to me," he would tell himself.

And now, there they were throwing a big homecoming celebration for his kid brother, Ted. The guy who takes off for New York City to become an actor, loses everything and shows up at their doorstep again.

Ted, the actor! Well, he was well-suited for the part. He was always acting. Pretending. Posing. Anything to get his way and finance his latest get-rich-quick scheme. Internet stocks. Day trading. Offshore accounts. And there was Dad, throwing money behind him and his wild ideas. Wasting his hard-earned cash on a loser who couldn't even graduate from technical school. "I'll pay you back, Dad, I promise," Ted would say each time he pocketed some more of Dad's dough.

Yeah, right.

Dusk settled over the estate. Inside, the party was getting wilder and wilder. Jerod could see his brother and his dad slam-dancing their way through the living room. *Doesn't Dad have any dignity?*

He's embarrassing the whole family! thought Jerod. *Well, he'll wise up soon enough. He'll be back out here any minute begging me to come in. He owes me that much.* Then, he shouted toward the house, "Even if I have to wait here all night, I'm not coming in there! I'm not going to a party for my brother! Do you hear me?!"

But of course, with the music playing, no one did.

And so, as night began to fall, the people inside the house laughed and danced and partied on. And Jerod stood there alone on the deck, with his arms folded across his chest and his teeth clenched. Staring angrily at the open door.

And no one at the party even missed him.

CHECK IT OUT...

This story is based on the most famous story Jesus ever told. We usually call it the story of "The Prodigal Son" (the word "prodigal" means "wasteful.") Most people think it's a story about the younger brother, the one who came home. But, think again. It's also about the one who refused to come in. Read it for yourself in Luke 15:11-32.

THINK IT OUT...

Jesus left his story unfinished. We never find out if the older brother joined the party or stayed out on the porch fussing about his father's forgiveness. Lots of people are like that older brother. They didn't run from God; they just drifted. Slowly. While living in the same house. And they've even convinced themselves that they're the ones who deserve a party. And all the while, the doors are open and God is inviting them inside. Inviting us inside.

LIVE IT OUT...

This story has a lot of meat to it. It's about the rebellion and restoration of the younger brother; the love and forgiveness of the dad; and the bitterness and resentment of the older brother.

To apply this story, you gotta think about where you're at with God. Which person are you most like right now? Which brother are you—the one who ran from God, or the one who drifted? Are you in a foreign country? Are you standing on the porch? Or are you in the arms of your heavenly Dad?

PRAY IT OUT...

God, I know at some times in my life I've been like the younger brother running from you, and at other times like the older brother drifting from you. Sometimes I come in and repent, but most times I stand outside and resent. Today, change my heart. I know forgiveness can only come with a change of heart, and even that's a gift from you. It's all about your grace. Forgive me, Dad. Wrap your arms around me again. I wanna come in to the party, Lord. I don't wanna be left out in the cold. Amen.

15

THE MOST UNUSUAL KINGDOM OF ALL

The Kingdom of God is like . . .

A Mustard Seed . . . (Matthew 13:31, 32)

Elmer and Bufus carried their buckets into the room and gazed at all the fancy switches and knobs.

"Wow!" said Elmer. "This place looks like one giant computer!"

"You see that button, Elmer?" said Bufus. "That's the one!"

"That tiny little red one?" asked Elmer.

"Uh, huh," said Bufus. "That's the button they told me not to push."

Bufus leaned his mop against the wall and scratched his head. "I wonder why they'd say that, Elmer. It doesn't look all that important. I mean, it's just one little button."

"I know. But they said not to push it."

They looked at each other.

They looked at the button.

They looked back at each other.

"Why not?" said Bufus, shrugging. "What'll it hurt?"

So, he pushed the button and they waited. At first they heard nothing. Then, slowly, a low rumbling sound echoed in the room. Both janitors glanced at each other, grinned and plopped down into the rocket's seats. And they buckled up.

After all, once the ignition button has been pressed, there's no turning back. The only thing left to do is strap yourself in, sit back and enjoy the ride.

It's time to blast off.

. . . it starts small, but once it gets moving there's no stopping it.

Yeast in a Batch of Dough . . . (Matthew 13:33)

In the department store near the ladies' dresses, they sold the perfume.

70

One lady after the next would walk up, spritz some on her wrist or into the air in front of her and sniff.

Ahh!

And the funny thing was, even after she walked away, whether or not she bought any perfume, that whole area of the store smelled elegant.

Even people who hadn't sampled any for themselves could smell the aroma when they walked past the dresses.

Because the fragrance lingered in the air.

. . . everything it touches is improved by its presence.

Buried Treasure . . . (Matthew 13:44)

Katie took another bite of cake and ice cream. "So tell me again why your Dad is throwing this party?" she asked with her mouth full.

Andrea grinned. "Well, he lost his car keys and then my brother found them!"

Katie just shook her head. "But I don't get it! Why would he throw such a big party after just losing his keys!?"

"Not *losing* them, *finding* them. And the answer is, well . . . he's into parties."

Katie shrugged her shoulders. "Whatever. . . . But there's one thing I still don't understand. . . . "

"Yeah, what's that?"

"Why did he go and *hide* them again?"

Andrea just smiled. "Cause my dad loves to party. And my brother loves to search."

. . . you can't help but get excited when you find it.

A Pearl Merchant . . . (Matthew 13:45)

Adrian had been to dozens of shops. Everyone told him that he really didn't have to search so hard, that any old engagement ring would do.

But when you love someone as much as Adrian loved Ariel, there is only one thing to do.

Keep searching.

And then one day, after months of searching, he found it. The perfect ring. But the price tag was beyond anything he'd ever imagined. How could he afford it?

He couldn't, of course.

Adrian couldn't afford to buy the ring.

But knowing how precious Ariel was, he knew he couldn't afford *not* to buy it.

And so, when he sold everything he owned (including the shirt off his back) and presented the ring to her, everyone else just laughed at him. "What a fool!" they said. "He could have gotten by with a much cheaper ring! And at least then he'd have something to wear to the wedding!"

But Adrian just smiled. "She's worth everything to me. This is just a small way of showing her how much I love her."

After all, love makes you do stuff like that.

Still, everyone laughed. "Sure, she's precious to you, but to give up everything for her? To sacrifice *everything*? That's a little extreme, isn't it?"

Yes. It is.

Very extreme.

. . . it's worth the price, and it's worth the wait.

A Fishing Net . . . (Matthew 13:47-50)

The first day of volleyball tryouts, 45 girls showed up.

They all wore the same clothes. They all looked like players. They all knew lots of stuff about volleyball. But some of them had already become ineligible because of their grades. A few were smoking pot secretly in the locker room. And one girl was pregnant, but didn't even know it yet.

So, after taking a careful look at their grades and spending a little time getting to know each girl, the coach didn't have to cut anyone from the team.

They cut themselves.

And by the end of the season, only a handful of girls remained.

But you should have seen them play.

. . . not everyone who looks like a member really is, but

leave the sorting up to God.

New Treasures as Well as Old . . . (Matthew 13:52)

"The best salsa is always aged. The longer you keep it in the basement, the more fire it has!"

Yeah, but the best chips are always fresh. The longer you keep them out, the more stale they become.

"I guess the secret is bringing out the chips at just the right time."

Yeah, and having lots of salsa on hand so no one goes home hungry.

. . . if you liked the previews, just wait until opening night.

A Thief Coming At Night . . . (Matthew 24:42-44)

"Be sure you don't look away from the water!" cautioned the head lifeguard. "You must watch carefully every second you're on duty. If you don't, someone could die!"

The new lifeguard thought to herself, "I'll do just what he says." And she did. She was careful and watchful and observant and rescued several people her first summer of work.

And so, over time, she was promoted until she become head lifeguard at a nearby pool.

And she told her new lifeguards the same thing she'd heard all those years ago. "Someone's life is in your hands," she said. "You must be careful and watchful. The moment you look away, someone might go under."

But that day when she was guarding, she thought, "I don't need to watch the pool every single second I'm on duty. I'm experienced enough to know just how long I can look away without endangering anyone's safety."

And that very day, a little boy drowned.

. . . when you least expect it, expect it.

CHECK IT OUT...

Jesus had a lot to say about the kingdom of God, especially in Matthew 13:24-52. Go ahead and read it. Then, read the summary of all Jesus' kingdom talk in Luke 17:20, 21. Where is God's kingdom actually located?

THINK IT OUT...

Why would Jesus say the kingdom of God is within you? Isn't that kind of weird? What was his point? What would you sacrifice to get it for yourself?

God's kingdom is unexpected, worthwhile and precious beyond knowing. Is it in you? If so, are you prepared for the thief to return? Like that lifeguard, you're on duty. Be ready. Be watchful. Don't let it slip by.

LIVE IT OUT...

Who knows what Jesus would compare his kingdom to today: A wedding reception? An awards banquet? A slumber party? A parachutist stepping out of an airplane? A smile passed around the room? A news alert that the war is over? That feeling you get when you sink the game-winning free throw with no time left on the clock?

Actually, there are reminders of it everywhere. Today, try and think like Jesus. Look around you and find five things that remind you of God's kingdom. Then tell someone what you noticed.

PRAY IT OUT...

God, help me see evidence of your kingdom everywhere I look. In the eyes of children. In the clouds above. In the wrinkled laugh of an old man. But most of all, in a heart of faith and a life of love. I wanna live the kingdom life. It's more like an amusement park than a sanctuary. More like a birthday party than a teacher's lecture. And that's my kind of kingdom. Amen.

16

THE BACKSTAGE PASS

Hello, Radio Land! It's me—Rob "the Slob" Thompson! You're tuned to the Muck! 101.8 FM WMUK! Your source for muck 24 hours a day! I hope you're planning to join us for the White Venom concert Saturday night. Good luck getting tickets, though! They're going on sale at noon and you'd better be in line already or you're gonna be left out in the cold while we're rocking with the band. Now back to the music. Here's their latest #1 song, "Slither Low"!

As soon as he got home from class, Cole plopped down and punched away at the keyboard of his computer. "C'mon! I gotta get tickets!" he whispered to himself. "They can't be sold out already!"

It was 3:05 P.M.

He checked site after site after site. No luck.

"I knew they'd go fast, but not that fast!" he thought. 30,000 tickets, sold in three hours. It had to be some kind of a record.

As soon as he went offline, the phone rang.

It was his friend Daryl. "What's going on? I've been trying to get through!"

"I was online. What's up?"

"Did you hear about the concert?"

Cole sighed. "Yeah, It's sold out, man. I can't believe it! I even checked online. Nothing."

"Hey, what did you expect?" said Daryl. "It's White Venom! They're the hottest band in the country!"

"So, you didn't get tickets either—"

But before he could finish his sentence, he heard Rob "the Slob" come back on the radio. "Hang on, Daryl, they're making an announcement on the Muck—" He held the phone up to the radio so Daryl could hear.

Hey, White Venom fans! The concert is sold out. You heard it here first—sold out! That's the bad news, but the good news is we've got

*you covered. I've got one front-row ticket to give away. Not only
that, but our winner will ride a chauffeured limo to the concert
where he'll hang backstage with the guys from the band before the
show. Then, after the concert, it's party time until dawn. E-mail us
your name and phone number in the next 30 minutes and we'll
choose our lucky winner sometime tomorrow. Stay tuned and be
ready. You gotta be listening to win and the announcement could
come at any time. And now, back to the music!*

Cole gasped. A front-row seat, limo ride and backstage party with
the band!

"Did you hear that, Daryl?" he shouted. "I gotta hang up so I can
e-mail 'em my name right away!"

Cole slammed the receiver down and started typing. Five minutes
later he'd registered his e-mail address for the contest. And to make
sure they could reach him, he left his cell phone number instead of
his home phone. "That way, they can get in touch with me at work
tomorrow," he thought. "If I win."

And that night, he hardly slept. Tomorrow was the day of the contest! He was so excited he put his cell phone right next to the bed in
case they called early in the morning.

But he didn't take the time to plug it into the recharger.

And the next morning, he took the phone with him into the bathroom while he took a shower. He carried it with him to breakfast. And
he kept it in his pocket when he went to work at the coffeehouse.

And he waited. All day he waited. He tuned his radio to the Muck
and listened. But they didn't announce anything about the contest.

*I hope to see you tonight! It's gonna be awesome! We'll have the
guys from the band in the studio today at 3:00 P.M. for a little interview. Be here or be there, but don't miss it!*

Huh.

No word. No news. Nothing.

"Maybe I was just dreaming the whole backstage party thing up,"
he thought. "Or maybe they gave it away to someone else already."
He was so discouraged, he turned off the radio even before the White
Venom interview was over.

76

Finally, at 5:00 P.M. he headed home. Discouraged. Tired of waiting. He didn't even notice that his cell phone had already been dead for two hours.

When he turned down his street, he met a limo coming from the other direction. "Huh, there goes the lucky winner, now," he mumbled.

But then, when he stepped inside, the light on his answering machine was blinking.

"You idiot! You moron! This is Daryl! Where are you? They called your name, man! You won! Rob 'the Slob' has been trying to call you for the last hour! They sent the limo to pick you up!"

What?!

Cole ran to the window. The limo had just turned off his street. He could see it getting onto the overpass a few blocks away.

Oh, no!

"I can still get in," he thought. "I just gotta get down to the concert in time!"

He bolted outside, jumped into his car and took off. *He'd won a free backstage pass to a White Venom concert! It was unbelievable! This was a once-in-a-lifetime opportunity! And he almost let it slip by!*

The streets were packed with cars going to the concert. But he finally made it to the rear side of the coliseum.

He pulled up next to the White Venom tour bus and hurried over to the backstage door. A man the size of a lowland gorilla stood in front of it with his arms crossed over his huge chest. "I'm sorry, I can't let you in there."

"Yes, you can! I won the contest!" shouted Cole.

"What contest?"

Cole sighed. He could hear the band members laughing and tuning their instruments just on the other side of the door. They were only inches away from him!

"I'm Cole Buchanan. I won the WMUK backstage party. I get to hang out with the guys from the band and then party with them in a limo all night long!"

"Just a minute, kid." The gorilla man pulled out a walkie-talkie and whispered into it. He nodded his head and then stuck it back on his belt.

"Well?" said Cole impatiently.

"Sorry. No one in there has ever heard of you and I don't have your name on my list. And if your name's not on the list, you don't go in the door."

Cole was yelling now. "You gotta let me in! You have to!" He ran for the door and yanked at the knob. It was locked. He felt the ape man's hand on his shoulder.

"No!" cried Cole. "I've waited my whole life for this moment!"

But the ape man wasn't listening. He just picked up Cole and tossed him against the concrete wall.

"I said you can't go in," grumbled the gorilla. "Now, go home before I have to hurt you. Permanently."

Cole gulped, looked up at the size of the man and slowly walked back to his car.

So that night, as 30,000 fans rocked the night away, Cole was stuck at home, listening to the Muck.

And the next day, he took a hammer and smashed his stupid cell phone into little bitty pieces because it hadn't gone off when Rob "the Slob" called.

But even that didn't make him feel any better.

CHECK IT OUT...

Read Matthew 25:1-13. Notice that in Jesus' story, all the girls got tired of waiting—even the ones who were prepared. Jesus emphasized over and over that no one is gonna know when the end of time arrives. No one. So, be prepared! Don't give up waiting. There isn't gonna be time for a second chance. Once the door is closed, no one else gets in. No one. Period.

THINK IT OUT...

How can you stay ready for Christ's return? What do you need to do to get prepared for the concert? Are you ready for it right now?

In Jesus' story, the wise girls had to buy their oil. It cost them something. What's it gonna cost for you to be ready? A few friends? Family? Wealth? Popularity? Are you willing to pay?

LIVE IT OUT...

Can a once-in-a-lifetime opportunity be lost because of carelessness? Jesus seemed to think so. If you're a follower of Jesus, there's no off-season. No vacation time. It's an all-out, to-the-edge, no-turning-back, extreme-thing that requires consistency, faithfulness and readiness. Are you interested? Don't get caught outside pounding on the door when the concert of all time begins!

PRAY IT OUT...

I'm gonna be honest, Jesus. I get tired of waiting. I get tired of waiting for you to answer my prayers, to work in my life and to come back to earth. But I know your timing is always perfect. And you want me to be ready. Prepared. That means when I hear that little voice that says it's okay to take some time off from being faithful, I need to say "no." And I need to say "yes" to you instead. Oh, and by the way, thanks for the backstage pass to eternity. I'm looking forward to the party. Amen.

17

PASSING THE ENTRANCE EXAM

As they walked into the room, Stanley whispered to his friend, "Hey, Fred, did you study for this?"

Fred shook his head. "No, I didn't even know there was gonna be a test!"

"What?" asked Stanley. "How could you not know?! I've been cramming for this thing for years! You wanna get in, you gotta pass the entrance exam! Everyone knows that!"

"I didn't," said Fred.

Stanley just shook his head. "I hope you make it, dude. . . . I'd be lonely without you."

The teacher appeared at the front of the room and began motioning for the students to take their seats. "Stanley, you can have a seat there, by the heater," she said. "And Fred, sit up here by my desk."

Stanley watched his friend walk up toward the teacher's desk. "Man, he's dead meat," he thought. "She probably made him sit up there because she thinks he's gonna cheat!"

Then, once all the students had been seated, she handed out the tests. "Now, as all of you know, this is a timed test," she said.

Stanley grinned as she handed him his exam. "Hey, this should be easy!" he thought. "There are only six questions!" He snatched up his pencil and got right to work.

#1 - Whose picture was on the latest cover of "Faraway Missions" magazine? (Hint: It was a five-year-old Ugandan girl.)

Hm. . . . He'd expected some questions on world hunger. He'd even read the standard textbook on agricultural economics while studying for the test. . . . But he hadn't thought of hunger in terms of real people! Sure, he subscribed to "Faraway Missions" Magazine. He always left it out on the coffee table of his apartment so people could see it. . . . But he had no idea whose picture it was. "I'll just make up some foreign-sounding name," he thought.

#2 - Who was the boy you cut in front of at the water fountain on your way into this room today?

Huh? He couldn't remember cutting anyone off at the water fountain! Oh, wait. . . . Yeah, he'd shoved that little kid with the runny nose out of the way . . . but how was he supposed to know what the kid's name was! A ball of sweat began to bead up on Stanley's forehead. "I'll just skip that one for now and go on to #3."

#3 - What was the real *name of the kid you used to make fun of in the hallway on the way to your sophomore geometry class? (You know, the kid you called Peanut-Head.)*

Stanley just stared at his paper. What kind of a question was that? How was he supposed to remember! That was two years ago! "Hm," thought Stanley. "Let's see . . . Peanut-Head . . . Peanut-Head. . . . Yeah, I do remember him! We used to lock him in the gym lockers during lunch. . . . But what was his name . . . ?"

Stanley had no idea.

#4 - What's the name of the homeless lady who lives under the overpass two blocks from your house?

"What's with all these name questions?" he thought. "I didn't know there'd be so many names!" He tried to remember if he'd ever even met a homeless lady near his house . . . Hm . . . Oh, yeah. There was that one lady he walked past every day on his way to work at the bookstore. But come to think of it, he'd never once even talked to her.

He looked around for a minute to see how everyone else was doing. Some students were busily scribbling on their papers. But most looked as bewildered as he was. "I wonder if they got the same questions I did," he thought.

#5 - What is the first name of the 84-year-old man who lives in Room 211 of the Oakridge Care Facility on Cleveland Avenue?

"This is insane!" thought Stanley. "How am I supposed to know that! I'd never be caught dead in an old people's home! Sick people make me uneasy!"

#6 - How many times have you visited your Uncle Luigi in the last 18 months?

"What?! My Uncle Luigi has been in prison for the last 18 months!

Who wrote this test anyhow?"

He finally wrote something down for each of the answers and put his pencil down. He carried his test up to the front of the room and set it on the pile of exams. Everyone else was already done. As he walked past Fred, he murmured, "How do you think you did?"

Fred just shrugged his shoulders. "I don't know. . . . Okay, I guess. It seemed too easy."

"Huh," thought Stanley as he returned to his seat. "He must have gotten another version of the test."

Finally, the teacher stood up and made an announcement. "Well, I've looked over your tests and I've got the final grades right here. A couple of you made it in."

Stanley grinned. Finally, the moment he'd been waiting for.

The teacher continued. "Fred, you can come with me. The registrar would like to talk to you. . . . I'm sorry, Stanley, but you didn't pass."

"What! I know I got that last one right!" yelled Stanley. "The answer was zero! I've never visited him!"

"I know," she said.

"But what about the other five questions!?" Stanley continued. "What were the answers to those!"

The teacher just smiled and said, "Me."

"What!" screamed Stanley. "You! But you work *here*! How could you be in a nursing home and the inner city and Uganda and my geometry class!"

"I get around," she said. "And I'm a master of disguise."

Fred stared at her with a look of amazement on his face. "Wow! I had no idea it was you this whole time! I didn't even know!"

The teacher smiled, "I know, Fred, we studied your transcripts. You always completed your daily assignments right on time."

So that day Fred went to meet with the registrar. And Stanley was dismissed from class.

CHECK IT OUT...

There's an exam coming that you can't cram for. Read about it in Matthew 25:31-46.

THINK IT OUT...

What do you think Jesus *really* meant when he said, "You did it for me"? Could he have meant what it sounds like he meant? How would that change how you look at people you meet every day? How do little things (like looking after the sick, feeding the hungry or visiting those in prison) really matter?

In God's eyes, showing compassion and meeting the physical needs of those less fortunate than you is a practical way of expressing your love for Jesus. You actually serve him when you serve them.

LIVE IT OUT...

Did you notice that the righteous people in Jesus' story didn't realize they were serving the king? They didn't expect to be honored. They'd passed the test without even realizing it!

What if you don't run into homeless people, prisoners or starving orphans every day? Is it possible to still care for them? How? Will you start being more careful to complete your daily assignments from now on?

PRAY IT OUT...

Hey, God, I'm not sure how to say this, but . . . I've walked past you and ignored you and slammed my door in your face. I've cut in front of you in line and watched you go hungry and homeless. I'm sorry. Help me change so that my life reflects your kind of love and compassion. Amen.

18

SECOND CHANCES

Even through the door, Tara could hear them.

It wasn't the first time she'd listened to her parents arguing. And after what happened today, she knew they'd be talking. But still, it hurt to hear the words.

"I just can't deal with her anymore!" said her dad. "Do you know how many times we've been through this?! I'm sick and tired of cleaning up her messes! She hasn't changed, Marge. I'm telling you, she hasn't changed!"

"Keep your voice down, Carl," said her mother. "I don't want her to hear us."

Tara stared at the ceiling where the shadows were. Shadows. That's what she wished she was. A shadow. Then maybe she could just fade away unnoticed. She'd let her parents down so many times. Maybe her dad was right. Maybe she was a hopeless case. I mean, he was right about one thing—she hadn't changed. She kept having the same problems.

She rubbed her hand against her stomach. She was down to 89 pounds but still felt like her stomach was too fat. She felt a tear forming in her eye. Tara fingered the bottle of pills. Last spring she'd failed. She always failed. But tonight, she would do one thing right.

"We should give her another chance," her mom said.

"Another chance!? How many chances does this girl get? She'll just try starving herself again! Or maybe slitting her wrists like she did last April! None of the counseling has helped one bit. And how long has she been doing this? Three years! She collapsed at gymnastics practice today, for goodness' sake!"

"Carl, I think we need to be there for her now. I think she's ready to make a change. We need to support her. Let her know that we love her."

Tara listened carefully.

Her dad seemed to stumble over the words. "You're right, honey. I . . . I . . ."

What was that? Was he crying? Tara leaned closer to listen.

"I just love her so much and I don't know what else to do anymore."

"Let's pray for her." It was her mom talking. "Let's pray for us."

And then, all Tara could hear were whispers.

She got up, walked into the bathroom and closed the door. She locked it and stared at the bottle of pills.

Love? He really still loved her even though she'd failed him so many times?

"If they're giving me another chance, I'm taking it," she muttered.

Then, she flushed the whole bottle of pills down the toilet and headed downstairs for supper.

● ●

Dylan was kicking the soccer ball around the field when his coach walked up.

"Hey, Coach! What's going on?"

"Dylan, I need to tell you something."

"What is it, Coach?"

"I'm not starting you this Saturday in the game against Lancaster High."

"But why not?" gasped Dylan.

Coach Cox sighed. "You just haven't been producing, Dylan. I need to see more points out of my forwards."

"Coach, c'mon. Gimme one more chance. One more game. Please! I promise, you won't regret it! I know I haven't been playing my best, but I'm ready for this game. I really am. Please!"

Dylan's coach was quiet for a long moment. Finally, he said. "All right, Dylan. You get one more chance. But if you mess up, you're sitting the bench. . . ."

But that Friday night, there was a party. And when one of the neighbors called the cops, Dylan got busted for underage drinking.

And when Coach Cox saw him the next day at school, he just shook his head. "I give you another chance, and this is how you act? You're not only not starting. You're off my team."

"Wait, Coach! Wait!" called Dylan.

But Coach Cox had already turned and walked away.

CHECK IT OUT...

Read Luke 13:1-9. This is a story about grace, second chances and God's just judgment. Jesus repeats himself twice (verses three and five) and then tells a story with the same point. What will happen if we don't repent?

THINK IT OUT...

Are you more like Dylan or Tara? How would you describe how they responded to the second chances they got? Did Dylan deserve to start? Did Tara deserve to be loved? What does that tell you about your relationship with God?

An apple tree is supposed to produce fruit. A storm cloud is supposed to bring rain. But what is a *person* supposed to produce? John the Baptist put it best in Matthew 3:8, "Produce fruit in keeping with repentance."

Repentance produces a changed life. So, change your mind. Repent. If you're unrepentant, you're fruitless. You deserve to be "cut down and thrown in the fire."

LIVE IT OUT...

God is a God of second chances. And third chances. And more chances. Chance after chance after chance. Lots of chances. How many? That's up to God. But someday there won't be another chance. That's the point of Jesus' story.

So don't put it off. If you need to make a change, do it today. If you need to take care of business with God, do it now. Today is your day to change. While you still have a chance.

PRAY IT OUT...

Fruitless. That's how my life has been. I need a change. I need you to work something radical and different in my life. I don't want to just stay here, rooted to the ground, but not producing anything at all. Make me alive. And help me produce the right kind of fruit. Amen.

19

JOINING THE ROAD CREW

Yeah, the Road Crew has an important job, alright.

We're the ones responsible for making sure all the correct signs are in place along the side of the highway. You've probably seen us hard at work surveying the land, digging the holes and putting up the road signs. We're pretty important people.

I remember when I first started working for the Highway Department. "We've got all these important signs to put up," they told us. "And you'll all have to work together to do it. Some of you will be diggers, others droppers, still others levelers or painters. It's vital that people see these signs! If they don't, they'll end up crashing in a ditch! Go therefore, and reach all highways, putting up signs in the way we have commanded you, and lo, your supervisor will be with you always, to the very end of your shift."

So, away we went. To the suburbs, and in all the little villages and townships and to the very ends of the county.

We took our signs to the streets and began to place them everywhere we went.

But it didn't take long for us to notice that only a few people paid any attention to the signs. Most people hardly gave them a second glance. They didn't even slow down to let us work! Some people made fun of us. And a few even threw garbage out the window at us as they zoomed past.

Just putting up the signs wasn't working. We needed a new strategy.

So we tried painting the signs fluorescent colors, surrounding them with flashing lights and making them bigger and bigger until they were the size of billboards. But it seemed like the fancier the signs got, the less people paid attention to their message.

We recorded CDs of Road Crew members singing about the signs, and we opened up roadside stands to sell books about building materials and T-shirts with signs printed on them. But even the stores, slogans and "Contemporary Construction Music" didn't convince many people to follow the signs.

Finally, we started staging little dramas by the side of the road, showing what would happen to people if they didn't obey the signs. Car wrecks. Body bags. Fake blood. Pretty graphic stuff. And that worked for awhile . . . until the plays became so predictable that people just watched the first couple of minutes and then drove away without staying until the end.

I was so frustrated I even put up three "Stop!" signs in the middle of the road so people would have to maneuver around them. But they just drove right over them.

Once I even dragged this little old lady out of her car and started beating her over the head with a speed limit sign. "Can't you read? Slow down and turn around or you're gonna crash! Can't you see this is a dead-end street?!"

But the only thing that earned me was a lawsuit. Still the people didn't pay attention.

That's when I started to take it all personally.

I figured that they weren't just rejecting my signs, they were rejecting me! So I started working even harder, putting in extra hours and even reading signs aloud through a megaphone to people as they drove by.

Because of my hard work, I was soon promoted to supervisor of one of the crews. It was great! Finally, I could do whatever it took to get people to obey my signs.

I ordered my men to follow up with everyone who made a U-turn. We'd pull them over and instruct them on the meaning of every sign we knew. We invited them to Driving School and encouraged them to join a Driving Club as soon as possible.

Sometimes, I made my men stay up all night. We worked on holidays and weekends and gave up a little family time. After all, this is Road Work! What could be more important than that? Of course, some workers burned out. They just quit and headed home.

But they were the ones who weren't cut out for Road Work anyway.

Now, don't get me wrong. There were always a few people who read and followed the signs. But we felt it was our job to get *every* motorist to obey them all the time.

Yeah, we were the hardest working crew of all. Not like some of those *other* crews.

There's this really liberal crew on Second Avenue that started changing the signs. They turned all the "One Way" signs into "A Way" signs since, according to them, there are lots of ways to get to your destination and it doesn't really matter which road you take.

They changed the "Yield" signs into "Resist" signs because they didn't like the idea of having to slow down to let someone else go in front. They took down the "Detour" signs and put up a very helpful sign that read, "You're Never Lost as Long as You Think You're Going in the Right Direction."

And they got rid of the "Speed Limit" signs all together. "After all, limits are so . . . well, limiting," they said. "The important thing is to make motorists feel good about how they're driving, regardless of how fast they may be going or what direction they're heading!" All the warning signs went as well. You know, things like, "Caution," "No Passing Zone" and "Merge."

Eventually, the only signs they allowed were flowery placards that announced how much the Highway Department cared about everyone's safety.

And, of course, there were more accidents than ever on that side of town.

Some of the people at the Highway Department didn't like all the changes—the liberal crew's or mine. "Your job is to put up the signs," they said. "Not change them or try to make people obey them. Just do your job and go home at night and sleep tight knowing that day and night people will be reading those signs."

What kind of an attitude is that? If these signs are supposed to have a life-and-death message, I can't just *let* people obey them, I need to *make* people obey them! It's not their fault if they disobey, it's mine! After all, I'm a member of the Road Crew!

I know of only one crew that does things the way the Highway Department recommends. They stick up their signs and move on. I talked to their supervisor once.

"We just believe that if someone obeys the 'Yield' sign, he'll eventually begin to obey *all* the signs. It's natural. You can't stop it."

Huh. Who ever heard of anything so foolish? Just put up your signs and leave the rest to traffic patterns?! Trust the signs *alone* to change people's driving habits?! Seems like an awfully lazy attitude if you ask me.

I've watched that crew. They spend a lot of time with their families. They take weekends off, go on yearly vacations and spend holidays relaxing and enjoying themselves. What a bunch of losers!

Not that I resent them. I just think they lack the dedication needed to do the job. They just don't have what it takes to be a committed Road Worker. Like me.

And, yet, for some reason, there don't seem to be as many accidents on that side of town as there used to be.

Hm. I just don't get it.

CHECK IT OUT...

Mark 4:26-29 is the "Tale of the Seed that Grows by Itself." It's so short that it's easy to overlook at first, but it's an incredibly important little story.

THINK IT OUT...

Why do you think Jesus emphasized that the seed grew by itself? Have you ever met someone in "the ministry" who felt it was his job to do God's job of conversion? What happened to him? What happens to a seed that is watered too much? How do some church people water others too much?

It's interesting that when Jesus healed people, he often told them, "Don't go and tell anyone." Yet, they did. And when he left the earth to go to Heaven, he told his followers, "Now go and tell everyone." Yet, we don't.

When is that gonna change?

LIVE IT OUT...

Lots of times Christians think it's their responsibility to convert people. But think again. It's the Holy Spirit's job to convict, convert and then comfort. We're simply there to get the message out. There's no need to get stressed. God's Word will have results. That much is guaranteed. See for yourself in Isaiah 55:10, 11. See the similarities between this passage and the story Jesus told? Do you think he was thinking of it when he told his tale?

How do you evaluate success in serving God? Well, if conversion is God's job and not ours, success doesn't depend on the size of our churches, or the number of decisions or baptisms we get. Success is being faithful. Leave the results up to God.

PRAY IT OUT...

God, it's okay to take a break, to relax, to sleep. Sure, it's important to live a life for you and witness to others about what you've done. But you're the one who makes your kingdom grow. Sometimes in ways that I don't even understand or comprehend. I'm here to plant, to wait, to watch and to harvest. You're the one who makes people grow. Help me do my job and stop trying to do yours. Amen.

20

CRYING OVER SPILLED COFFEE

Okay, so Justin knew he should have been more careful. Especially in a ritzy upscale restaurant like Alberto's. Especially since he had barely enough money with him to pay for the meal. But he was trying to impress his date and the vases didn't look that fragile and he had no idea they were from the 13th century Ming Dynasty in China. Whatever that meant.

And he was usually pretty good at juggling.

But when he missed the handle on the first one it threw his rhythm off and all three of them went crashing to the floor.

Oops!

Everyone for tables around gasped and turned to stare.

"It's okay," he said, blushing. "Nothing to see here!"

He glanced over at Nikita and tried flashing his winning smile. She didn't look as impressed as he'd hoped.

"Justin, you just broke their vases!" she squealed. "And I don't think they picked those up at a rummage sale!"

He gulped. This was not looking good.

Just then, the manager arrived. He stood there, just staring at the shattered pieces of his priceless vases on the floor. It had taken him a lifetime to earn enough money to buy them.

"Um, sorry about that," said Justin.

The manager didn't move. One of the servers leaned over and whispered to Justin, "Do you realize that each of those vases cost more than Guatemala's Gross National Product!"

But the manager was still silent.

Justin realized this was much worse than he thought. "Listen, I've got this really cool comic book collection and it's all yours for the asking. I'm not sure how else I can pay you back."

Finally, Alberto sighed. "You can't pay me back, young man. So I shall not ask you to. Please enjoy the rest of your meal. Compliments of the house."

Now, that was unexpected.

All the people who'd gathered around to see what had happened, stared in shock. Then, they gave the manager a standing ovation.

Finally, Justin just sputtered, "I don't know what to say!"

Nikita leaned over and whispered in his ear, "Say, 'thanks.'"

"Thanks," said Justin.

"You're welcome," said Alberto.

Justin offered a few more times to pay for the vases, knowing that he'd never be able to. But the manager shook his head and smiled and walked away.

"What a deal! Can you believe that!" said Justin, once Alberto had left. "He forgave me! He even gave us a complimentary meal! Amazing!"

"He is a very generous man," said Nikita.

They ordered their meal and sipped their water and watched as a crew of servers efficiently swept up the broken vases and deposited them into the garbage can.

A few minutes later, their food arrived.

But just then, as Justin was about to dig in, the maître d' turned too quickly and the platter of roast duck he was carrying on his shoulders tilted slightly and a cup of warm coffee tipped off.

It teetered there on the edge for a moment—just like in the cartoons when someone runs off a cliff and then lingers there in midair kicking his feet.

Then, it fell through the air and landed right in Justin's lap.

You could have heard his scream from the other side of the restaurant. He didn't scream because it was too hot, just because it was so wet.

"What are you doing? You imbecile! You moron! What have you done?" Justin leapt to his feet and brushed at his jeans. There was a large circle of brown liquid on his right thigh.

"I'm sorry, sir. It was a mistake. I'm so sorry," sputtered the maître d'.

"Mistake, my foot! You've ruined a perfectly good pair of jeans. This is coming out of your paycheck!"

"But, sir—"

"Don't talk back to me!" screamed Justin, grabbing the maître d' by the throat. "You spilled coffee on my jeans!" And he shook the man so violently that it looked like the poor fellow's head might just fly off.

It took two retired bankers and a lady wearing a mink coat who knew karate to free the maître d' from Justin's grip.

Well, of course, some of the people watching were the same ones who'd been there for the vase incident. They called for help and once again Alberto arrived. This time, flanked by several police officers.

"What's going on here?" he asked.

"This stupid waiter spilled coffee on my pants!" yelled Justin. "They cost me $20 at Wal-Mart!"

Alberto looked at the coffee stain. "I see. I think I'm beginning to understand."

"Good! Then you'll fire this waiter and pay for these jeans to be dry-cleaned!" hollered Justin.

"No, I won't," replied Alberto.

"What!"

"Officers, this man owes me some money. As well as a comic book collection. He broke three of my priceless vases earlier this evening."

Uh, oh.

"What are you doing?" asked Justin. "I thought you said you weren't gonna make me pay!"

Alberto just smiled. "I changed my mind."

And as they dragged Justin away, the maître d' straightened his collar and went back to work.

And the people applauded for Alberto once again.

CHECK IT OUT...

Peter wanted to be fair. He figured that forgiving someone seven times for a sin would be pretty merciful. Doesn't that seem reasonable? What if your pastor had seven affairs? Would your congregation still forgive him?

Jesus would. Look at how he answered Peter's question in Matthew 18:21-35. Look at those last two verses. How does God treat us when we don't genuinely forgive others?

THINK IT OUT...

What's the point of Jesus' story? Should you keep track of how many times someone sins against you? If not, what should you do instead? Where's the limit of forgiveness?

It's pretty shocking that someone could be forgiven so much and yet forgive so little. Could it really happen like that?

Actually . . . yes.

We've been forgiven so much, yet we're hesitant to forgive others. We're a lot more like Justin than Alberto.

If God treated us fairly, we'd all be in Hell already. Thank God we don't get what we deserve! Every breath we take is a gift. God's forgiveness is full, complete and everlasting. We need to both accept his forgiveness and then extend it to others.

LIVE IT OUT...

Every Christian has been pardoned for a crime we *did* commit. Lots of crimes. Day after day.

So when someone sins against you—spreading rumors to ruin your reputation, lying to you, cheating you of what's rightly yours, how do you respond? Would you even forgive someone for purposely setting you up for a crime you didn't commit? What if it sent you to death row? Jesus would.

Jesus did.

His forgiveness is always available. That's what mercy is all about—not getting what you deserve.

PRAY IT OUT...

Father, the way you forgive me is astounding. You don't keep track of my wrongs, instead you wipe them away. How? How can you treat me like that? Teach me to forgive like you do. So freely. So willingly. So deeply. So often. Amen.

21

MASQUERADE

The Student walked into the mask factory.

A slick-haired man behind the counter smiled and launched into his little sales speech. "Welcome to Masks-R-Us! Your source for masks both new and used! Can I sell you a mask today, son? Here's a nice model. We call it the 'GOOD STUDENT WHO KNOWS ALL THE ANSWERS' mask."

"No, I don't think so," said the Student.

"Hm . . ." said the man, holding up another mask. "This one's popular with people your age! It's called the 'I'M TOTALLY COOL AND QUITE POPULAR' mask. What do you think?"

The Student shook his head. "No, actually—"

But the man just smiled. "Okay, let me guess . . . you want something a little less showy. . . . Well, I've got only one copy of this mask, but it's yours for the asking. . . ." He held it up and announced: "The 'ALL-AROUND NICE GUY' mask!"

"Um . . . You sure have a lot of nice masks, sir. But actually, I was hoping to turn this one in. . . ." The Student pointed to his face. "I've decided not to wear a mask anymore."

"Not wear a mask?!" the man gasped. "But everyone wears masks! If they didn't, I'd be out of business! I can't take your last mask!"

The Student turned to leave. "You sure you don't want it? It's in pretty good shape."

The man sighed. "Let's have a look at it."

The Student slipped off his mask and handed it across the counter. It felt good to take it off in front of someone, even if it was only a stranger.

"Hm. A 'PERFECTLY HAPPY LITTLE CHRISTIAN WHO NEVER DOES ANYTHING WRONG' mask. . . . I don't get too many of these. Most people hang onto them for a lifetime. Are you sure you wanna part with it? I mean, if you don't wear a mask, people won't always be impressed with you. . . . They might notice your faults. . . . They might even see you cry."

The Student nodded. He'd thought of all that already. "Yeah, but I'll finally be able to laugh," he said. "*Really* laugh."

"You won't look your age anymore. You'll look more like a little kid!"

"I know."

The man grunted. "How much do you want for it?"

"Nothing. You can have it. I'm just glad to be rid of it," he said. And then he opened the door and stepped outside. He blinked a little in the bright sunlight, but then smiled and let the door swing shut behind him.

And there, in the store, the man grinned as he put the Student's old mask on the shelf near the cash register. "I'll sell this one right away," he said to himself.

And you know what?

He did.

CHECK IT OUT...

Jesus valued children. He held them up as examples of humility, trust and innocence. And he said to enter his kingdom you had to become like one. Read Matthew 18:1-6.

THINK IT OUT...

One thing is for sure, "childlike" faith doesn't mean "childish" faith. Children trust fully. They laugh. They giggle. They cry. They let you know when they need a hug. They haven't learned to hide or doubt or question as well as we have.

What do you think Jesus meant when he said we need to become like little kids? What masks do you like to wear? Do people even know? Who has seen you without any masks on?

LIVE IT OUT...

Kids live life one moment at a time, just like Jesus did—never putting it off, never hiding from it. What about you? Have you been shoving your dreams and joys and regrets into some dark corner of your heart and then covering them up with a mask? Do you think maybe you'll come back and deal with them later? Do you?

God knows what we look like without our masks and he loves us anyway. Right now, think of your three favorite masks. It takes a lot of courage to remove them. But when you do, you start on the journey back to being a kid again in your Daddy's arms.

PRAY IT OUT...

I've given up some innocence, God. As I've grown up, I've grown less and less like a child. But that's not what you want. I've seen things. I've done things. And rather than taking them to you, I've shoved them into the closet of my heart, hoping somehow they'll disappear. But they don't. Clean out my closet, God. Remove my masks. Free me to trust in you like a child again. With honesty, transparency and humility. Amen.

22

A Cinderella Story

Happily ever after.

That's how my grandma always used to end the stories she told me at bedtime. No matter how bad things got, the princess would marry the heroic prince who'd slain the dragon. They'd inherit a castle in a peaceful kingdom and then live happily ever after.

In story after story after story.

But as I grew older, it didn't take me long to realize that real life doesn't always work like that.

Grandma died when I was in third grade. And there was no one there to tell me bedtime stories anymore.

Then the next year, my parents got a divorce. It was really messy. Arguments. Fights. Accusations. And after Dad walked out, he never called home again. Ever. So I ended up living with my mom and her boyfriends. I lost count of how many there were. None of them stayed very long.

Finally, mom and I moved in with this guy who used to drink a lot. At first, I'd just hide in my bedroom to get away from him. But then, when I was about 12 or so, he started following me in there. Those were the worst times of all.

One night, he got so drunk, he held me on the floor and put out his cigarette on my neck. I screamed and screamed and screamed. And my mom just stood there, watching.

Grandma used to tell me monsters aren't real. But they are. I know that now. I used to live with one.

So I started wearing a scarf around my neck. To hide the scars.

And all during that time, the kids at school were talking about me. I heard the words they used. I didn't even know what some of them meant, but I had a pretty good idea.

So then, when I was 14, I ran away. From everything. And I spent the next few years on the streets.

It was a hard life. You have to survive. A girl has to eat. So, I sold everything I owned. And then I started selling the only thing I had left. Myself.

One man after the next. But there was no love. Not from them. Not for them. The men used me and I used them. And love doesn't use people. That much I knew, because my grandma had loved me. And all she did was give.

And through it all, I never took off the scarf.

But then, last October, I met him.

He was working at the soup kitchen I sometimes stopped at. He handed me a plate of food.

He wasn't the kind of man you'd expect to meet on the streets. Most men I met kinda peered at you out of the corner of their eyes. They all wanted the same thing. But he stood tall and smiled at you and listened to you. As if what you had to say really mattered. And I had no idea what he wanted.

"Hard night?" Those were the first words he said to me. And it sounded like he actually cared.

"I'm fine," I said. I didn't need anyone feeling sorry for me.

But he didn't turn away.

"How much?" he said.

"How much what?"

"How much does it cost?"

I remember thinking, *Huh. Just like the others. I'd thought maybe you were different. But I guess not.* And I have to admit, I was disappointed.

"That depends," I said. "What did you have in mind?"

"I thought maybe we could spend some time together."

"How much time?"

"All night."

I quoted him a price and he nodded. He reached into his wallet and pulled out the money. Cash. Up front. It was more than I'd made in t̶ ̶ ̶ ̶ast six weeks.

̶ ̶ ̶ ̶ ̶ got a place I usually go," I said.

̶ ̶ ̶ ̶et's go to my apartment," he said, smiling.

So we left.

He took my hand and started talking with me. Not to me or at me. *With me*. He asked about my childhood and my favorite toys as a kid. We walked past a park and he pushed me on the swing in the moonlight. I laughed as I soared toward the stars. I couldn't remember the last time I'd laughed.

It was really weird. But I kept thinking, *I wonder what he wants from me?*

As we left the park, we walked past a grocery store.

"Do you like ice cream?" he asked.

"What?"

"Ice cream," he repeated. "Do you like it?"

"I haven't had ice cream since I was a kid," I muttered.

"You're still a kid," he said. And at the time I didn't know exactly what he meant. He bought a gallon of it and we spent the night sitting on his couch playing board games and eating chocolate chip cookie dough ice cream.

He bought me *ice cream*. Can you believe it?

Then, when it got late, he led me upstairs to his bedroom. And I knew the time had come. "There's the bathroom in case you want to take a shower," he said motioning toward a door. "I'd like to take you out for breakfast if you like. Is 8:00 good?"

I looked at him. He was telling me he wasn't gonna spend the night with me. "What kind of game are you playing?" I asked.

"No game," he said. "Good night."

And he went downstairs and slept on the couch.

The next day we ate breakfast together, and then, he asked me to meet him at the park to fly kites that afternoon. "If you need money, I'll pay you," he said. "Just don't go back to the streets tonight."

I was tempted to, but I didn't. I didn't know what to say. It was like I was learning to be a kid again. Like a secret part of me that had been buried beneath all the junk in my life was breathing again.

Is this what loves feels like?

Then the snows came. And winter is a hard time to be living on the streets. But he took me out on a deserted street and asked me to dance. So we danced right there in the night as the snowflakes fell lightly on our shoulders.

And during the dance, my scarf pulled loose. I should have been more careful because that's when he noticed.

"You've got scars," he said.

Quickly, I looked down, flipping the scarf back around my neck. "Yeah," I muttered. "I'm damaged merchandise." I didn't mean to say it, it just sort of tumbled out. It was the term one of the men had used when I told him my price. "I'm not paying that much for damaged merchandise," he'd grunted.

I stared down into the snow. But then, he brushed the flakes off my cheek and leaned forward, pulling back the scarf. And he kissed my scars. Gently. He touched my past and accepted me despite who I'd been. Despite what I was. And then, even though it sounds unbelievable, I felt the scars disappear. They faded from my heart. They vanished. And I knew that I loved him.

My heart broke that night. But not from sadness, his love broke me and set me free. I finally believed it was possible to be loved.

"I'm so sorry," I whispered.

"For what?" he said.

"For what I am."

"I'm not ashamed of you," he said. "I love you." And he unwrapped my scarf and tossed it into the snow.

I guess, maybe fairy tales can come true after all, when you truly believe.

CHECK IT OUT...

In the stirring story recorded in Luke 7:36-50, Jesus offered forgiveness and acceptance to a lady whom Luke discreetly called "a woman of the streets." In other words, she was the town whore. And she wept over her sins at Jesus' feet.

Jesus didn't turn her away. He wasn't embarrassed to be seen with her. He accepted her. He forgave her. He loved her.

THINK IT OUT...

Did you notice Jesus' question to the Pharisee? He didn't say, "Which of the two would be more *thankful?*" He said, "Which would have more *love?*"

You don't generate love for Jesus by feeling good about yourself. It's exactly the opposite. The more clearly you see your sin, the more you'll love your Savior. The more you're forgiven, the more you love. That's what Jesus said.

The Pharisee felt good about himself. The woman didn't. Do you try to grow closer to Jesus by feeling good or by admitting your sin? According to Jesus, only one technique will work.

LIVE IT OUT...

Look again at Luke 7:50. Faith and love and forgiveness go hand in hand. Each grows out of the other. You always serve the ones you love. Naturally. Love changes you into a servant. There's no other way about it.

Have you done anything for God today simply because you love him? Just because of love? How has forgiveness changed *your* life?

PRAY IT OUT...

Dear God, sometimes I try to generate love for Jesus by feeling good about myself. But it doesn't work that way! The bigger my need, the greater my love. So God, this is kind of a weird thing to pray for, but show me my sin. Make it real. Reveal my debt. Show me how much I've failed you so that I can begin to love you more deeply. Just like the woman did. Amen.

23

NIGHT OF THE VIRUS

(ring, ring)

"Yes?"

"I'm sorry to call you this late at night, sir, especially on your private number . . . but I think we've been hit by the Mudola Virus."

"That new computer virus they're been talking about on the news?"

"Yes, sir."

"But how? I thought we had antiviral software?"

"Well, we do, but whoever invented this is very clever—a real pro. He made it past all the firewalls and security codes. He must have broken our access code sometime last night after everyone left the office. When we turned on the system today, we saw evidence we'd been hacked. We have no idea who could have done it."

"I do. One of our competitors. Probably that group from Silicon Valley. They're big into corporate espionage."

"What do you want us to do about it? The Web guys told me they don't have a clue how to get rid of it."

"Well, what exactly does this virus do?"

"It imitates the programs you already have running and slowly eats up your memory. As far as we can tell, it doesn't affect any of the programs we already have installed; it just takes up space. But over time, it might affect all our programs. It's hard to say at this point. The computer still can't tell which programs are infected."

"It doesn't sound that bad. . . . What about our files?"

"It looks like they're safe, but the thing is, sir, when you try to delete the virus, that's when the problems start. It writes itself onto some of the unaffected programs. When you kill it off, it takes the good programs with it."

"Hm. So, our operating system is safe?"

"Well, for the time being . . . yes. It appears that way. But—"

"Okay, then I'll tell you what to do: Don't do anything."

(long pause)

"You still there?"

"*. . . I'm sorry, sir, I must have a bad connection or something. For a moment there, I thought you said we shouldn't do anything.*"

"You heard me right."

"*But, sir—*"

"Listen, if you start randomly deleting files, you might end up deleting ones that haven't been affected. Right?"

"*Well . . . yeah. It's likely we wouldn't be able to tell which files were corrupted until after the deletion process—*"

"There you go. That's the last thing I want. Now, the Mudola Virus won't spread, right? It won't destroy our current software?"

"*Not that we know of—*"

"Okay, we're planning to upgrade to a new system next month, right? So just leave the infected programs in there until then. When we upgrade, we'll screen all the programs, dump the ones that've been ruined and save the good files in a new drive."

"*But sir, the virus might spread! It's taking a huge risk just leaving it in there!*"

"If it'll help protect the software we're using, I'm willing to take that chance."

"*But—*"

"I'm much more interested in protecting the good programs than removing the bad ones. Whoever did this expected us to be reactionary, to respond without thinking. But we're gonna be patient instead."

"*So, what'll I tell the Web guys?*"

"Just tell 'em their boss decided to wait."

"*What about the hacker?*"

"Oh, don't worry. I'll find him. And I intend to prosecute. Believe me, whoever did this is gonna pay. He'll serve time, that much is for sure. . . ."

(long pause)

"*Sir?*"

"Yes?"

"*One more thing.*"

"What's that?"

"A few years ago they tried to recruit me—our competitors in the Valley that is."

"And?"

"And I'm glad I stuck with you. I like your management style a lot better."

"Thanks. I'm glad you stuck with me, too."

(click)

CHECK IT OUT...

If Jesus retold his story of the wheat and the weeds today, he might retell it like this. Read Matthew 13:24-30, 36-43 to find out how he did tell it 2000 years ago.

Jesus explained that in his story, the field represents the world. And there are sons of the kingdom and sons of the evil one. One day, the sons of the evil one will be destroyed and the sons of the kingdom will be rewarded by being taken into his house.

THINK IT OUT...

Q – Why is there evil in the world?

A – It was engineered and designed by Satan. He sent it our way to destroy us.

Q – Could God remove evil from our world?

A – Of course.

Q – Then why doesn't he?

A – It wouldn't benefit us as much as we think it would.

God's answer to why there is still evil in the world is this: removing it might harm believers. It's that simple. We grow up side by side with evil because God loves us so much he isn't willing to remove it . . . yet.

Our roots intermingle. Our influence is felt. Both the wheat and the weeds grow stronger until the harvest. We're never gonna get rid of evil. But God will. And his day is coming.

LIVE IT OUT...

Are you trying to uproot yourself from all the "weeds" of the world? Or are you growing up side by side, with your arm around someone who needs to hear about Christ? Rather than recoiling from our culture, we should grow up within it, impacting it for God.

Evil will rise, but it will not win. Christians need to resist the urge to uproot and go replant themselves in soil surrounded only by other wheat. Side by side with evil. That's God's way.

That's how Jesus did it, remember? He faced angry crowds, was betrayed by a buddy and watched his friends desert him. He was falsely accused, beaten, tortured, mocked and killed. Yeah, Jesus knows the results of evil firsthand.

He faced it head-on. And then he conquered it.

Justice is coming. Our job is to keep growing until then.

PRAY IT OUT...

God, it's sometimes hard to understand why bad things happen, why evil exists. The world seems to grow more violent every year, with school shootings and terrorist attacks and abortionists murdering helpless babies. But you've promised that as evil grows, so will good and the evil will not overcome it. I'm here. Use me as an influence to plant good in the world. Help me put my arms around someone who needs to see your love in action. Side by side. Until you come back. Amen.

24

THE PARABLE OF THE GOOD SKINHEAD

Lateesha knew it wasn't a good idea to walk through that neighborhood at night. Especially since she was young. And female. And alone. And African-American.

Just last week two kids had gotten gunned down on their way home from a football game. But she'd lost her bus pass and didn't really have a choice.

She pulled the collar of her jacket up and trudged through the snow.

She didn't see her attackers until it was too late. They'd been hiding in the alley next to Bingham's Meat Market. And they were on her before she even realized what was happening.

"No!" she screamed, but then her scream was cut short by the hand clamped across her mouth. Before she could struggle free, her attackers had taken her purse, ripped off her jacket and yanked off her skirt. They punched her in the face and neck and slammed her against the frozen ground. And they kicked her in the head and back with their steel-toed boots.

Just then, a car turned down the street and one of the men said, "C'mon, let's get outta here, man!"

She felt one final kick in the gut before they ran off and left her to die in the alley.

Lateesha was hurt very badly. She could feel the blood soaking her hair and saw a widening pool of red next to her head.

That's when she heard someone coming.

"Please! Oh, please help me!" she called.

It was a nun. One of the Sisters of Charity, an order committed to helping the poor and homeless people who roamed these streets.

"Oh, good!" thought Lateesha. "I'll be safe, now."

But when the nun saw how badly she was hurt, she just hurried on her way. After all, the criminals who did it might still be in the area. There was no sense endangering herself to help someone who probably wouldn't survive anyway.

The night grew colder and colder. Lateesha felt her legs getting numb. "I'm dying," she thought. "I'm bleeding to death."

That's when her pastor appeared. He'd been invited to speak at an inner-city revival and was already running late.

"Pastor Richardson! It's me, Lateesha!" she called.

Oh, he recognized her voice, but he just ignored her. He didn't have time to stop right now. Maybe he could stop on the way home, if she were still there.

By then, Lateesha was barely conscious. So when she heard the footsteps crunching the snow near her head, she was only able to turn and groan.

A man was stooping down next to her.

"Oh, my goodness!" she heard him say. But she wasn't listening. She was staring wide-eyed at his black leather jacket covered with swastikas and racist slogans. Things like, "Equal Rights for Whites!" and "Niggers, Get Out!"

"Oh, no!" she thought. "This guy is a neo-nazi Skinhead! He's probably gonna rape me and leave me for dead!"

But he wasn't leaning down to hurt her. He was taking off his jacket and wrapping it around her. He removed his Ku Klux Klan baseball cap and pressed it against her head to stop the bleeding, and then he lifted her up gently.

She couldn't tell how far they walked, but it seemed like forever before the sliding doors eased open and the bright lights of the emergency room hurt her eyes.

"What happened to her?" she heard someone ask.

The Skinhead just shook his head, "I don't know. I found her like this over by 42nd Street."

The doctors helped him place Lateesha onto a gurney and then asked him to wait in the lobby. Which he did.

A few minutes later, the police arrived and began to question him. Of course, no one believed his story—that he just happened to find a half-dead, half-naked girl in the snow and decided to carry her 14 blocks to the hospital. Especially since she was black.

He already had a police record and had been charged with assault and battery two months ago. He'd been found "not guilty" back then, but everyone knows what kind of people those skinheads are.

And besides, in court a nun and a well-respected pastor both testified that they'd seen him in the vicinity of the victim and that he "looked like he was up to no good." Lateesha herself admitted, "I didn't really see who attacked me. . . . I guess it could have been him."

And so, the Skinhead was found guilty of attempted murder and attempted rape and was sent away to state prison for a good long time.

And the citizens of that city felt much safer now that he was off the streets.

CHECK IT OUT...

Jesus told the story we often call "The Good Samaritan" when he was questioned by a religious expert. You can find his story in Luke 10:25-37. The theologian wanted to justify himself for not loving his neighbors. Jesus told the story to shock and confront him. Do you think it worked?

THINK IT OUT...

Did you expect this story to end the way that it did? Why or why not? How did you feel at the end of the story? What made you feel that way?

Both Jesus' story and this one have a lot to say about priorities. What was the most important thing to the nun? The pastor? The Skinhead? What was the most important thing to Lateesha? What's most important to God? Why do we so often think "someone else will stop to help so I don't need to"?

LIVE IT OUT...

In Jesus' story, we learn not only who our neighbor is, but what love really looks like—it's costly, inconvenient and risky. You may not find someone dying by the side of the road, but you can show compassion to people, too—even those of another culture, race, background or religion. Think of two people you know who are hurting (not necessarily physically) and commit to go out of your way to love them this week.

The only way to overcome prejudice is love, working itself out in little ways. One person at a time.

PRAY IT OUT...

God, sometimes I've been like the first two people who walked past without stopping to help. Sometimes I've turned my back on people who are getting picked on or made fun of. At the lunch table. In the hall. After class. But those are the people I should care the most about! God, give me the courage and compassion to reach out to the unlovable and show them your kind of love. Like the Skinhead and the Samaritan did. Amen.

25

WHY I DON'T WORK AT GONZO'S ANYMORE

When we got the new manager at Gonzo's Rib Barn, things began to change right away. Because not only was he the manager, he'd also bought the place. So he could run things any way he wanted to.

At first, it was cool. He gave us each a raise, cut down on our hours and poured money into fixing up the place. That was awesome because under our previous manager, it'd become a real dive. But now, it was the talk of the town.

With the higher morale came better service. And with better service came more customers. People started driving in from miles around to eat at Gonzo's. Then we had to hire more servers, more cooks and more shift managers.

And that's when the troubles started.

You gotta understand, I'd been around there since the beginning—ever since Gonzo's first opened its doors four years ago. I was the first one to pull a rack of ribs out of the oven. I was the first one to use the cash register. I was the first one to squirt a customer with barbeque sauce.

So anyway, when we got the new manager, I was really thrilled. I thought. *"Yeah, we're gonna be the next big thing! Franchise City, here we come! And with my experience and track record I'm headed for corporate headquarters!"*

Well, I was half-right.

We did grow. Fast. Within the first six months under the new management, we were able to open up two other franchises across town. And soon, those were bursting at the seams, too.

Which meant even more staff.

Well, I started getting a little curious. I mean, I know we didn't have a very wide profit margin. So I started wondering, *How is this guy able to keep the employees so happy while still growing so quickly and not going bankrupt?*

Then, one day I overheard a few of the new staff talking. "Can you believe this job?" one of them said. "This is the best deal around! I've only been here two weeks and I'm already making $22 an hour!"

"Huh," says the other guy. "That's what I make, too."

At first, I thought it was some kind of trick. Or weird joke. So, I walked right over there and asked the second guy. "How long have you been working here?"

"About two months," he said.

"And you've been here two weeks?" I asked the other guy.

"Uh, huh."

"And you're both making $22 an hour?!"

They both nodded. "Yeah. Go figure! What a deal!"

"That's what *I* make!" I yelled. "You shouldn't be earning as much as me! I've been here since the beginning! I have more restaurant experience than *anyone*!"

"Except the manager," said the guy who'd been there two weeks.

"Oh, go barbecue some ribs!" I said. I was pretty steamed alright.

I figured it was time to set the record straight. You know, get things out in the open. So I had my friend in the accounting department go through the records. Sure enough, there was no mistake.

Everyone on the payroll got the same salary. It didn't matter how long they'd been there, how many hours they worked or how well they'd done on their performance reviews! It just wasn't fair!

So I decided to complain to the manager.

"What's going on here?" I said.

"Payroll records are confidential," he said. "You shouldn't be nosing around in there."

"Yeah, yeah, I understand all that," I said. "But it's just not fair! You're giving everyone the same paycheck each week! Regardless of their responsibilities or experience or anything!"

"Hm . . ." he said. "So, you think I should pay some people more money?"

"Of course!" I yelled.

"People like . . . you?" he said slowly.

All of a sudden I didn't like where this conversation was going.

But I wasn't about to back down. "Yes! People like me!"

"Are you happy with your paycheck?"

"Of course," I said. "At least I was until yesterday when I found out how much you're paying everyone else!"

Then he started giving me this line about how if I got a fair deal I had nothing to complain about. And since it was all his money anyway, if he wanted to give it away and be generous to some people that was his right. Yeah, whatever.

I deserve more!

Then he gets really serious. "Are you asking me to give you what you *deserve*?"

"Exactly! That's precisely what I want!" I said the words before I'd even realized what I was saying. They seemed like the right words to say at the time. I mean, in a moment like that you just say how you feel, and that's how I felt.

"Okay, then. You're fired."

"What!"

"You're fired. You looked through confidential financial records. That's illegal. You wanted me to treat you fairly, to give you what you deserve. I'll be pressing charges of course, just like you requested. Good-bye. Please don't slam the door on your way out."

"But that's not what I meant!"

But it was too late.

So anyway, that's why I'm here. Standing in the unemployment line filling out this stupid job application for a minimum wage position at Waldorf's Pickle Factory.

And wondering where I'd be today if I'd just kept my big mouth shut.

CHECK IT OUT...

When a sports team wins a championship, everyone gets a trophy, whether they were starters or not. When a political candidate is elected to office, everyone who voted for him feels good, not just the ones who were on his campaign committee. If you and your friend both get a CD that was on sale, you both saved money, regardless of who bought the

CD first. Now, with all that in mind, read Matthew 19:30–20:16.

THINK IT OUT...

What did Jesus mean when he talked about the last being first and the first being last? How would you feel if you found out everyone at work got the same paycheck as you? Would you feel cheated or thankful? Why? What about Christmas presents? Do you ever feel cheated by comparing yours to someone else's?

Some people trust in Christ early in life and others later. But all Christians are saved by grace. So if Heaven is a gift, does anyone have the right to be resentful or jealous? How should we respond instead?

LIVE IT OUT...

We're experts at the comparison game. And we're quick to ask for things to be "fair." But in God's eyes, it's all about grace.

You wouldn't really want to tell God, "You weren't fair to me! You owe me!" You wouldn't really want to hear him say, "Okay, my child. You want me to be fair rather than gracious. . . . I can be fair. You want me to deal with you based on your works rather than my grace, I can do that. . . ."

It's like God is saying, "You got a good deal, didn't you?"

"Well . . . yeah."

"Then what are you complaining about?"

Live this week with an attitude of gratitude remembering that it all boils down to grace.

PRAY IT OUT...

God, thanks for grace. I'm sorry for being whiny sometimes. I'm just thankful there are so many people in your kingdom. Remind me daily that everything I have is because of grace, not justice. Thanks for not treating me fairly! Amen.

26

BURIED ALIVE

I used to think the worst fate a human being could have would be to get buried alive.

I mean, I'd heard these stories about how sometimes, in the olden days, they'd open up caskets and find fingernail scratches on the inside of them. The person had been in a coma or unconscious and then awoke after the burial.

Imagine what that would be like, trapped in a coffin with no escape. The air slowly running out. Hoarse from shouting. Fingers rubbed to the bone from clawing at the top of the casket. Pounding. Scraping. Screaming.

But, of course, there's no one there to hear you scream.

The thing that scared me most was the idea of waking up in there and having that sudden realization that you're six feet underground and no one is ever gonna rescue you. I couldn't imagine anything more frightening.

Yeah, I used to think getting buried alive would be the most horrible fate imaginable.

But not anymore. Now I know different.

There's one fate that's much worse.

● ●

I guess I should back up a little bit.

Up until a few days ago, it was life as usual. Get up, work out in my home gym, shower and shave, slip on my suit and head to work.

My firm provided e-technology for Internet service providers. In the last couple of years our stock had risen more than 2,000%. Not bad. Actually, pretty good. It provided more than enough cash for me to wear the finest clothes, drive the coolest sports car and live in a penthouse suite in L.A.

I rode the elevator downstairs, smiled at the bellhop to my building and walked outside onto the busy street.

And of course, there by the door sat Emilia—an old mentally-ill Mexican bag lady. You could tell by her clothes that she'd lived on the streets for a long time. Just one of the thousands of homeless people in my city. She'd chosen my building to panhandle.

She always had a smile as she reached out her hand. "Oh thank you, Mr. Artisan!" she would say. "God bless you! God bless you!"

And what can I say, I felt sorry for her. So every day, I'd hand her some loose change as I walked past.

I liked her. To a point. I mean, she was harmless enough. And I always felt good about myself when I gave her some money. Like I was doing my part.

My church did its part, too. We talked a lot about social issues and justice and caring about others and world peace. We held bake sales and potluck dinners and we sold candy bars so our youth could go to the amusement park. We didn't talk too much about Heaven and Hell and sin and forgiveness and all that stuff. It wasn't that kind of a church. "My God would never send people to Hell," I used to say.

But then, two days ago, when I came home from work and walked up to her, she didn't say anything. She just lay there staring unblinkingly at the street. No one else stopped. No one seemed to care that Emilia the homeless lady had died.

I felt bad, you know. But what could I do?

So I called the cops and watched them take her away. Then I went to bed like usual and, while I was fast asleep dreaming about my Ferrari and my next weekend ski trip, it happened.

I died.

You should have seen my funeral. Everyone was there. Businessmen and women. Actors and actresses. Even the mayor. Channel 4 News covered it. After all, I was an upstanding and respectable citizen. An entrepreneur. A philanthropist. Everyone looked up to me.

Yeah, I had it all. Money. Wealth. Power. Prestige.

And then I died.

And I woke up here.

It was just like my nightmares. The screaming. The desperation. The sudden realization that there's no way out. Trapped. That's the best way to describe it. Trapped without any hope of escape.

How was I supposed to know this is what was waiting for me?

At first I complained. "No one ever warned me. No one! It's not fair. Proof! That's all I needed! A little proof!"

But it didn't take me long to realize that even that was a lie. I wouldn't have believed even if there had been proof. Because I didn't want to believe—that would have required I admit I needed someone to forgive me. And I wouldn't have done that for anything.

And I guess, when it boils down to it, that's why I'm here.

Yeah, there is one thing worse than getting buried alive. Getting sent here and staying buried. Alive. Forever.

If you get buried alive on earth, at least you can look forward to dying. But here, you don't get that chance. Ever. There's no end to the agony. There's no hope for the future. And there is no way out. Solitary confinement that never ends. A fate much worse than death.

And the most horrible, unimaginable thing of all is knowing how content my family is at that church. How safe they feel.

And how soon they're gonna be joining me.

Rather than Emilia.

CHECK IT OUT...

Read Luke 16:19-31. Jesus told this story because the upper-class religious leaders were snickering at him. Because they loved money so much.

(By the way, this is the only story Jesus ever told about a real person, or at least the only story in which he actually mentioned someone by name. Because of that, many Bible scholars don't think it's a parable. They believe it's a true story. But whether or not it happened to someone Jesus knew, it happens all the time.)

THINK IT OUT...

Did Jesus refer to Hell as a real place? What difference would it make in your life if Hell were real? Why don't people want to admit that it is? Can you think of anything worse than being trapped forever in a place of suffering with no hope of escape?

In this story, we discover that in the afterlife we will still think, reason, remember, dream, care and feel. Think of five words that describe the Hell Jesus described. How does it differ from Heaven? Think of what it would be like watching your family members die off one by one and go to Hell. What would that be like? What can you do now to stop that from happening?

LIVE IT OUT...

Jesus really turned the tables upside down in his story. The rich man became the poor man. The healthy man became the suffering man. The man with good things got nothing, while the guy with nothing got everything. The businessman became the beggar. And the beggar became the king's own son.

Life is the length of a heartbeat compared to eternity. No matter how long you live, the day will come when there are no more second chances. And the only way to spend forever with God is to repent and place your faith in his message.

Don't end like the rich man in Jesus' story. His greatest regret was that his family would end up joining him in the place of suffering. It's a regret he had to live with. Forever.

PRAY IT OUT...

God, help me to see that eternity hinges on faith. When we die we will either be trusting in ourselves to get us into Heaven, or trusting in you and what you did for us. I ask, make that message so clear to me every day that I see this life through the eyes of eternity. With faith in you, I don't need to fear death. For it is really the pathway to life and freedom. Help me get the message out. Amen.

27

THE EDGE OF DANGER

"Emeral, this is awesome!" said Marcos Castillo, dipping his paddle into the water. "Thanks for inviting me to go kayaking with you. This is the coolest date I've been on in a long time!"

Emeral Davis smiled as she expertly twisted her paddle across the bow of her kayak and stroked it through the waves of Lost Peak River. Free equipment rentals were just one of the perks she enjoyed as a river guide for Outwater Expedition Specialists.

"Thanks. I thought you'd like it," she called back.

Their kayaks sliced through the crystal-clear water as the two teenagers paddled downstream. From a ledge on the cliff towering high above them, an eagle sent its cry echoing down into the quiet, remote gorge. But the stillness of the valley was deceiving. Only two miles away lay Chainsaw Falls.

They paddled in silence for a few minutes. Marcos wasn't sure if he should bring up the subject again. "Hey, I'm, uh, sorry about what happened at my house."

Emeral paddled in silence.

"I mean it."

Finally she answered. "It's alright . . . I guess. I just can't believe you were looking at that stuff."

Marcos followed Emeral between two rocks, remembering what had happened earlier that morning. His mom had shown Emeral to his room where he'd been on the computer and lost track of time.

"Hey, Marcos! Are you ready to go? The river won't wait forever!" Emeral pressed open his bedroom door.

Marcos fumbled for the mouse, but it was too late. She saw what was on the screen.

"Marcos, what was that?"

He managed to log off before answering. "Nothing . . . uh . . . Let's just get going."

"What do you mean nothing? I saw those pictures!"

"Hey, listen, it's no big deal, okay? It doesn't hurt anybody."

"Doesn't hurt anybody! It's disgusting! It degrades women and it warps the way men look at us!"

He'd spent the next 20 minutes trying to convince her it was the first time he'd logged onto that site.

Now, as he wove between the rocks trying to keep up with her, he swallowed hard. "Emeral, I was just surfing the Net, you know, and I decided to check out a couple sites I'd heard about. I thought they'd be restricted or something. But they weren't. It was really easy to get in. But I can control it, you know. I was just curious. I know when to step back."

Emeral didn't answer.

Suddenly she pointed her paddle downstream. "There it is," she called. "Chainsaw Falls. We get out here." She turned her kayak toward shore.

Marcos could hear the roar of the falls, but couldn't see anything. The river just seemed to end about 100 feet downstream.

"Whoa," Marcos said, gazing at the river.

"Yeah, whoa."

By now she had pulled her kayak ashore and was starting down a trail. "C'mon, I'll show you the falls."

But Marcos had another idea. What fun was it to look at a waterfall from the shore? He'd just paddle a little closer and then pull out farther downstream. He aimed his kayak into the middle of the river.

"Marcos, where are you going? Get back here! The current will suck you over!"

"I just want a better look! I'll meet up with you closer to the falls," he called back, edging his kayak into the current.

"Don't be an idiot! You could drown!"

Yeah, whatever, he thought. *I know when to pull back.*

Now the falls were only 50 feet away and the current was getting stronger.

"What's the danger of getting a little closer?" he hollered.

"Marcos! The current! It'll draw you in and it won't let you go!" It was tough to hear her now; the thunder of the waves engulfed her voice.

He'd been kayaking before. What made her the expert anyway? Just because she was a hot-shot river guide? He'd show her. He'd go right up to the edge and then turn around. No problem.

Out of the corner of his eye he could see Emeral bolting down the trail shouting to him. Wouldn't she be impressed when he pulled out at the very last second?

He could feel the tug of the current against his kayak. Easy now. He edged closer. Cool. It was only about 15 feet away. He could almost see the waterfall from here. Just a few more inches . . .

Suddenly, the water surged beneath him. Spray pelted his face and the kayak seemed to have a mind of its own. He slammed his paddle against the waves and desperately tried to back up. But it was too late. The current gripped his boat and lurched him toward the chute that funneled water over the falls.

Marcos's mind raced. *No! I didn't want to go over! I just wanted a closer look. No! No!*

The front of his kayak hovered above the eight-foot drop. He teetered for a moment and then plunged over the edge. Not even Emeral could hear him scream as the water swallowed his kayak and he disappeared.

"Marcos! Marcos!" By now she'd reached the base of the falls. She scanned the surface for any sign of him. How many seconds had he been under?

10, 11, 12 . . .

For Marcos, everything went black. He was choking on the water, blinded by sand churning in the current. He'd been tugged from his kayak and the water was spinning him around and around. Swirling him downward. Downward.

19, 20, 21 . . .

"Marcos!" Emeral wiped a tear from her face as she screamed at the river. "Marcos!" Suddenly, the river spit his empty kayak out of the water and washed it downstream.

"Oh, Marcos!"

26, 27, 28 . . .

Which way was up? Marcos was dizzy and weak. He didn't have the strength to swim anymore. He was being dragged to the bottom of Chainsaw Falls.

No, God! I don't want to die this way!

All of a sudden he saw light and his head broke through the water's surface. Marcos sputtered and gasped for air. Lashing at the water with his arms, he tried to stay afloat.

"Marcos!"

That's when he saw it. Emeral had tossed him a rescue bag! The rope was floating right in front of his face. He grabbed for it just as the water dragged him under again.

He could feel himself being pulled toward shore. Emeral was reeling him in like a fish.

Hold on, Marcos! Hold on!

Then his feet were on solid ground. He tried to stand, but collapsed. A hand helped him up.

"Thank God you're alive! I told you not to go near the falls!"

Marcos gasped, "I thought I'd be safe."

"It's never safe to go near the edge. By the time you realize you're in danger, you find you can't turn back, the current is too strong. That's what makes it so dangerous."

"Yeah, I guess you're right," he mumbled, remembering how, earlier in the day, he'd been lured into the current, one mouse-click at a time. And Marcos Castillo knew Chainsaw Falls wasn't the only thing he needed to turn back from before it was too late.

CHECK IT OUT...

The same person who taught his disciples to pray, "Lead us not into temptation," also taught them to *beware* of temptation. Read about it in Matthew 26:36-41.

Also, while you're in the book of Matthew, flip to what Jesus said about looking at pornography in Matthew 5:28. He doesn't beat around the bush, does he?

THINK IT OUT...

Marcos thought he could look as long as he didn't touch. But Jesus said that purity starts in the heart. Even that little glance can be full of sin. In God's eyes, every secret little sexual fantasy is just as wrong as having sex outside of marriage.

It's easy to point the finger at the weaknesses of others; but what sin do you like to flirt with the most? Lust? Pride? Anger? What entices you? What sin draws you in and wraps you in its lies and excuses?

LIVE IT OUT...

Jesus knew we'd have a hard time resisting sin. That's why he told his closest friends to "watch and pray." Because, even though they had a strong desire to do what was right (willing spirits), their natural sinful selves would lead them astray if given the chance (weak flesh).

Watching means avoiding those situations where the temptation will be the strongest. Praying means depending on God's strength instead of your own.

Jesus was tempted in every way we are (Hebrews 4:15), but never went over the edge. He never gave in, and because of that he's able to help us (Hebrew 2:18). Every day we're faced with choices. And each one will either draw us closer to God or lead us further from him. Turn to him right now and ask him to turn you around before the current pulls you over.

PRAY IT OUT...

God, I like hanging around the edge. I like to see just how far I can go without going too far. But the current usually grabs me and tugs me over. I guess that's why you warned us to watch and to pray. Forgive me for flirting with sin. Keep me pure in my body and in my mind. Keep me away from the edge of temptation. Amen.

28

MISSING THE MEAL

It wasn't your typical Thanksgiving meal. I mean, sure all the normal stuff was there—turkey, potatoes, stuffing, cranberries. But there was one thing missing—people.

Mom had spent all day baking. And, man, the house smelled good!

I was in the living room watching some college football when she called me. "Hey, Andy, go upstairs and tell your sisters it's time to eat!"

So I sighed, got up and jogged upstairs.

The first room I came to was Brianna's.

She was seated in front of her computer staring intently at the screen.

"Hey, Brianna, Mom says it's time to eat!"

Brianna clicked the mouse on one of the flashing icons in the corner of the screen. "Tell her I just found this really cool site about the cattle population growth in Venezuela in the mid-1800s and I want to check it out. I'll be down in a little while."

"It's Thanksgiving!" I said. "Can't that wait? I mean, you can surf the Web anytime; Thanksgiving comes only once a year!"

She just shook her head. "I'm serious! This site is so cool! And there's this thing for the first 100,000 people who sign up where you can enter your name to win a free order of small fries at Sizzle Burger! It's incredible!"

I just stood there thinking, *Why would you be interested in trying for a couple of fries when you've got a hot Thanksgiving Day dinner already prepared for you?* But, she wasn't budging so I shook my head and started down the hall. *Mom's not gonna be happy,* I thought as I knocked on Kendra's door.

"Hey, Kendra, it's time for supper."

No answer.

"Kendra!"

I knew she was in there because I could hear her singing along to a CD.

"Kendra, I'm serious, open the door!"

The door stayed close. "Quit bugging me, you little jerk!"

Yup, that was Kendra all right.

"Mom says it's time for supper!"

Silence.

"Kendra?"

Finally, the door flew open. "Tell Mom I'll be down later. I just got this new CD and I wanna listen to it before supper!"

"But Kendra! You can listen to that anytime! C'mon! Supper's ready!"

But she just rolled her eyes and slammed the door in my face.

Fine. I can take a hint. I went to the last room on the left. At least Brittany's door was open.

"Brittany?"

She put her finger to her lips and said, "Shh! I'm on the phone."

"It's time for supper. C'mon."

"Tell Mom, I'll be down in a few minutes. I'm talking to Curtis."

Curtis was her boyfriend. And if she was talking to him on the phone, it wasn't gonna be a few minutes. It was gonna be hours. Maybe days.

Then I had an idea. "Invite him to come over, too! I'm sure there'll be plenty of food! Especially if Brianna and Kendra don't come down."

But she just ignored me. And waved her hand at me to leave. So, I did.

I went back downstairs by myself.

Mom was setting the table when I entered the dining room. She'd pulled out the fine china and everything.

"Where is everyone?" she asked, pulling up a chair and sitting down.

I told her the whole story. How each of my sisters was too busy to come. And Mom just sat there for awhile. I felt kinda bad, you know. I mean, sure they'd been rude to me, but it was really Mom they were insulting by refusing to come downstairs. After all, she'd spent all day on the meal. And it wasn't like this was a big surprise or anything. I mean, they'd known all year that Thanksgiving was coming.

So, we just sat there and waited.

Nothing. No one came. The food was starting to get cold.

Finally, Mom glanced at the clock and shook her head. "Alright, if they won't come down for something to eat, let's take this food to the soup kitchen. We'll find someone who's hungry."

Huh? The soup kitchen! She had to be kidding! This was Thanksgiving Dinner! What was she planning to do, just give it away to some homeless bums?

"I think we oughtta just give it away to some homeless bums," she said.

"But, Mom," I said. "Don't you think we could store it in the fridge or something? I mean, they'll eventually get hungry and come downstairs!"

"It's Thanksgiving," she said simply, "a day to celebrate."

So that settled it.

She stood up and began boxing up the food. I helped her.

It took four loads to get all the stuff packed into the car. Then, as we walked out to the garage, she paused at the base of the stairs one last time. But it was clear they weren't coming down.

So, we hopped into the car and took off. My three sisters didn't even notice that we'd gone.

I'm not sure what they ate for supper that night. There wasn't much food left lying around the kitchen. Maybe they snacked on dog food or dug some scraps of orange peel out of the garbage disposal.

But I do know this—that night the homeless people celebrated Turkey Day with a feast. And no one went back outside hungry.

We had lots of leftovers, but we didn't take them back home. We took all that food to the streets and handed it out until every last bit was gone. After all, Thanksgiving comes only once a year.

And you wouldn't want to let a meal like that go to waste.

CHECK IT OUT...

God is a God of love, and love seeks to express itself. If someone refuses to accept his love, God will go out and search for someone who will receive it. Luke records Jesus' story of "The Feast for the Least" in Luke 14:15-24.

THINK IT OUT...

God's invitation is not to be taken lightly. He calls us for supper, and he won't drag us down the stairs kicking and screaming. He's not that kind of parent. Instead, he leaves the choice up to us. He's got grace to give, and if we don't want it, he'll search and search until he finds someone who won't turn down the invitation.

LIVE IT OUT...

How have you been responding to God's invitation? Do you scoff at it? Make fun of the messenger? Find other things to fill your time and your heart? In Jesus' day, it was a terrible insult to refuse someone's invitation to a feast. It would be like getting invited to a White House dinner with the president and saying, "No thanks. That's the night I have to clip my toenails."

God's invitation is for the feast of all feasts. The party of all parties. The invitation has been given. It's got your name on it. What are you gonna do?

PRAY IT OUT...

God, when I hear your call, your invitation to join you, I hesitate. There are so many other things I'd like to hold on to or take with me. But right now, here's my answer: "Yes." Before I even know what I may need to leave behind: people, power, passions or possessions. My answer is "yes." Now, tell me what you want me to do. Amen.

29

OUR NEW SALES STRATEGY

Memo: To all rookie sales representatives

From: Your Chief Executive Officer

It's come to my attention that some of you haven't been follow-ing company protocol while recruiting new clients. As a result, sales volume is down and the number of new independent consultants is on a sharp decline. Please read this memo carefully and follow it to the letter! As a review, here are our top four sales strategies:

Principle #1 - We Emphasize the Positive.

Explain how great our product is! How easy it is to use! How fab-ulous and carefree life will be when you finally buy into the program! How it'll give the consumer inner peace and spiritual fulfillment!

These characteristics will make people more interested in trying out the product. And that's what we want—product sampling. Let them nibble before asking them to take a mouthful. Little by little we'll draw them in until they realize they just can't live without us!

Never mention anything negative associated with the product. Sell the sizzle, not the steak.

Principle #2 - We Put People First.

Be sure to stress that, to us, people always come first. It's compa-ny policy! Show folks how we strive to bring families together. Remember, nothing is more important than pleasing the people you live with—not even our business. Explain all this before you ask peo-ple to sign on as consultants.

Emphasize that we don't create friction in families, but unity! Show people how little their lifestyle will change when they sign up and they'll be more apt to put their name on the dotted line.

If you mention how some of our sales consultants have lost inter-est and dropped out, gotten divorced because of their commitment, and even been mocked and killed, who would ever want to sign up?

Principle #3 - We Press People to Make Decisions.

Growth is more important than customer satisfaction.

We want to sell our product to as many people as possible as fast as possible. That means, you're always on the lookout for buyers. Never mind that you may never see this person again. Just sell! Sell! Sell!

Repeat customers are okay, but sales is the bottom line, not satisfaction. We'd much rather have 10,000 people buy our product today, than have ten people believe in our company tomorrow.

So, never walk away from someone and let them consider their options. Our competition might call our approach coercive, intimidating or manipulative. But who cares! We're salesmen, and it's our business to make people buy!

Remember, it's always better to be a little pushy to get someone to commit to a purchase agreement on the spot than let her walk away. Even if she hasn't had time to read the fine print.

Principle #4 - We Never Mention the Cost.

Always wait until the person has come forward to the checkout counter before letting him know how much the product is gonna cost. Only after they've committed themselves should they be told the price. That way, it'll be harder for them to back out. We want them to rush in. The more they think about their purchase, the more likely they are to say "no thanks."

Then, make it really tough for folks to back out of a purchasing agreement. Tell them not to worry about evaluating the payment options. Sure, other people may laugh at them if they overinvest in our company and go bankrupt, but never tell them that!

So, if you must bring up the cost, be sure that you make it sound reasonable, never out of reach.

And lastly, but most importantly, never ever mention that everything they own will become company property after they sign on. That's something they need to discover for themselves once we get them working here at company headquarters.

By then, they won't even realize how much they've actually paid.

Your affectionate CEO,

Beelzebub

CHECK IT OUT...

In Luke 14:25-35, Jesus told two stories about commitment, the "Tale of the Unfinished Tower" and the "Tale of the Terms of Peace." They wouldn't go over too well in many churches today, because our evangelism techniques are the exact opposite of Jesus' techniques.

THINK IT OUT...

If you're a follower of Jesus, did you count the cost? Has it gone like you thought it would? If not, was it because people recruited you with the wrong strategy? What does your evangelism look like—Jesus' strategy or Satan's? Why do you think that is? How can you change your approach so it's more like that of Jesus?

LIVE IT OUT...

Nope, Jesus wasn't a salesman trying to persuade people to enter God's kingdom. His approach made absolutely no common sense: explain the cost up front, emphasize the sacrifice rather than the benefits and freely let people walk away without embarrassing them or pressuring them to make a decision. There was no fine print.

Manipulation is the devil's tool, not God's. God warns and invites, but he does not entice. Jesus refused to force people into making a commitment. Instead, he encouraged them to carefully consider the cost. *"It's not an easy life, this life as a disciple. It's not comfortable. And it's not something you should just jump into. Look before you leap. Following me is gonna cost you. Find out what's expected of you before you sign on."*

But of course, the benefits far outweigh the cost.

PRAY IT OUT...

God, you were totally honest with people because you wanted them to know the truth. You wanted followers who were willing to give up family, possessions and even their own lives for you. Change my heart so that I let go of all the things that hinder my commitment. And help me follow your example when I invite others to become your followers. Amen.

30

THE DAY MY MOM CAME HOME EARLY

I knew I shouldn't have rented the movie.

It wasn't like it was from the curtained-off back room at the video store. You know the room I'm talking about. It wasn't that kind of movie. But still . . . it wasn't exactly the kind of flick you'd watch at church camp, if you know what I mean.

So, it's last Saturday afternoon and I'm home alone when Mom calls and says she's gonna be late. She needs to show a house to this couple from Maryland and won't be back until 8:00 P.M. She tells me to have a nice quiet afternoon and grab supper on my own.

Well, that gave me plenty of time to slip out to the video store. I figured I had plenty of time to watch it before Mom ever suspected anything.

So, there I am. At home. Alone. By myself. Lying on the couch. And I pop it in the VCR and start watching.

Some of the guys at school had recommended it to me and, well, what can I say? It was pretty much what I expected—pretty edgy stuff. I even pulled the shades shut to make sure none of the neighbors would see me watching it. You know, sometimes it's easier to watch stuff like that in the dark or late at night, when you know no one is gonna see you. It's not the sort of thing you watch when there are other people around.

Anyway, after only 20 minutes I was already surprised they were able to squeak it by with an R-rating.

And then, about halfway through, I'm getting hungry so I pause the movie and jog downstairs to grab a pizza from the chest freezer and when I come back up to the living room, you'll never guess who's sitting there on the couch reading the back cover of the video box.

Oh, man. I'm dead meat.

"Hey, Dave."

"Mom? What are you doing home?"

"Oh, the couple from Maryland never showed up and Robyn—you know, Melissa's mom—needed a ride home so I decided to come home early and join you for supper. And—what'cha' watching?"

"Um, nothing, Mom."

"Oh, come on. It says here . . ." and then she starts reading the back cover of the box. "'The erotic thriller of the year!' 'Smart, sexy, and suspenseful,' 'When desire takes control, there are no rules—'"

Say something quick before she reads the whole thing!

"Some guys at school recommended it. It's really not that bad; they just put that stuff on the back to try and get you to rent it."

Yeah, it was a lie. But I thought maybe I could convince her. Maybe convince myself.

So, she smiles a little, kicks her feet up onto the coffee table, and says, "Great! If it's not that bad, then let's watch it together. I'm kinda in the mood for a movie."

This is not good. Think, man, think!

"Uh, you wouldn't like it."

"Try me."

"It's got some, you know . . . like a lot of violence and stuff. I wouldn't want you to get sick or anything. Um . . . there might be some blood."

"I've had two babies. I should be all right." And then she looks at me all innocent-like. "Unless you don't want me to watch it with you. . . . You don't mind if I join you, do you?"

Man, she was persistent. I felt like screaming, "Yes, I mind! I mind an awful lot!" But I just stood there in shock holding the frozen pizza, which was starting to drip water onto my left sock.

This cannot be happening. This is not happening! My life is over!

She picks up the remote control, aims it at the TV and presses "play." "Better put that pizza in quick or you're gonna miss some of the show."

I wanted to tell her to wait for me, but I just shook my head, ripped open the pizza box, threw it in the oven and then returned to the living room.

"Here, Dave," she says, patting the couch next to her. "Have a seat. We'll have a little Mother-Son time."

For a few minutes the movie was pretty mild. Whew. Maybe all the really steamy stuff was over. Then, right after the chase scene with the helicopter and the one-armed skateboarder, the scene comes on. You know, *the* scene. The one all my friends had been talking to me about. And I just sat there.

I heard the timer go off telling us the pizza was done, but still I didn't move.

I was sure she was gonna ground me for a month, take away my snowboard and unleash one of those "Would Jesus want you to watch this movie?" lectures. Maybe her eyes would bug so far out of her head that they'd never fit back in again. I knew at least she'd gasp, blush and turn off the movie. At least that.

But she didn't. She just sat there. Watching.

And every moment that went by, I felt smaller and smaller and smaller.

That's when the smoke alarm went off.

"I think your pizza is ready," she says.

So I retrieve what's left of the pizza and we watch the movie all the way to the end.

Finally, after what seems like an eternity, the credits start rolling. "Hm . . . interesting. What did you think of that movie?" she says, grabbing a hunk of burned pizza.

And I just sit there feeling about the size of a paper clip. "What do you mean?"

"What'd you think? Did you like it?"

I figure it's some kind of parental trick questioning technique or reverse psychology or something. "I don't know. It was alright . . . I guess . . . I mean . . . it could have been better."

Brilliant answer, Einstein!

"Hm. . . ."

Okay, here we go. Settle in for the long haul. Lecture-orama about to begin. I knew it. I just knew she was gonna unload on me. She'd just been waiting until it was over so she could gather up all the ammunition available. I knew I'd never be allowed to rent another movie again. Until I was like 30 years old.

But she didn't say anything. She just stood up and said "Good night" and then went into her room. I almost wish she would have yelled at me.

Huh?

I sat there in shock for like half an hour.

If she would have lectured me I would have known what to do. I would have argued back. I would have made up all kinds of excuses. I would have pretended like I didn't know what the movie was really like, even though I did.

But she didn't say anything. And neither did I.

It was all pretty weird.

Just her being there made me uncomfortable. That was all it took.

Then, at school on Monday, I tell my friends that I'd rented the movie and my mom had walked in on me when I was watching it.

"And you're still alive?"

"Yeah, she actually watched the rest of it with me."

"Whoa! Cool Mom!"

I kinda nod. "Yeah, I guess she is."

Some of them are saying stuff like, "My mom would have killed me" or "My mom wouldn't have cared . . ." when Willy turns to me and grins. "So what did she say? Did she yell at you?"

Then everyone else is quiet and they're all staring at me. "She didn't say too much. Neither of us really liked the movie. We're . . . we're not into that kind of stuff."

And then I walked away.

And you know what?

It got me thinking. I started wondering what it would be like to live in a way that I never had to worry about when she might walk through the door. To live with nothing to hide and no fear of getting caught. That would be cool.

Yeah, I think I'm gonna give it a try. So I'm not doing anything I need to be ashamed of the next time my mom comes home early.

CHECK IT OUT...

The last few verses in the book of Matthew record an incredible promise that Jesus made to his followers. Read it in Matthew 28:16-20.

THINK IT OUT...

How would you feel if your mom plopped down next to you while you were doing something you knew you shouldn't be doing? Embarrassed? Weird? Ashamed?

Look at the verse again. Do you see that? Jesus said he would always hang with his followers. Never abandon them. Always stick with them.

Now, Jesus didn't promise his presence to freak us out. Or make us nervous. He wanted us to know he would always be there for us, not against us. And he wanted to comfort and encourage his followers.

LIVE IT OUT...

How do you act when no one is looking? If you think you can't get caught, do you do things you'd never otherwise do?

Character is how you act in the dark. When no one is looking. And even though no one else may see you, God will. You can't hide it from him. A life lived with integrity is one free from the fear of getting caught. Free from the fear of someone walking in on you. God wants us to live the same in the dark as we do in the light. Integrity has no private life.

That's the kind of freedom we find when we follow God whole-heartedly. That's the kind of freedom your friends will notice and want for themselves.

PRAY IT OUT...

Hey, God. Look deep into my heart. Expose those things I like to hide. Take me to a deeper level of commitment in which I don't do shameful things behind closed doors. You're always with me, not to look over my shoulder or shake your finger at me, but to encourage, comfort and strengthen me. I'm sorry for the secret things I've done and tried to hide from you. Make me a transparent Christian and unashamed follower of you. Amen.

31

THE BRAGGING BRICKS

The bricks near the top of the building loved to brag. "The mason placed us highest on the building, so we *must* be the most important bricks of all. After all, everyone has to look up to us! And we can look down on everyone else!"

And so, as they looked down on all the other bricks, they mocked those lower on the building by singing, *"Far up is a blessing and low is a curse, for higher is better and lower is worse!"*

They were quite proud of themselves, even though they weren't the world's finest songwriters.

Yet, through it all, the bricks near the bottom of the wall were silent. For they were too busy holding up the proud bricks to argue.

One day, an earthquake shook the village and the building began to crumble. Of course, all the bricks high up on the wall tumbled to the ground. They broke to pieces and split in half as they landed on the street, for they had fallen so far.

The only bricks that didn't break were the ones that had been at the bottom of the building—the ones that had borne the weight of the wall for so long.

So, when a crew of masons and construction workers arrived to repair the wall, they picked up those whole bricks that had been at the bottom and smiled. "Hey, look! These are still good! We can use them again!"

But the broken bricks were piled into an old pickup truck, taken to the landfill and dumped in a deep, deep pit.

And they did not sing their silly little song anymore.

CHECK IT OUT...

When Jesus noticed that some of his hosts liked to be honored, he told a short story to warn against pride before people. Read it in Luke 14:7-11.

Later, he told another short story in Luke 17:7-10 to warn against pride before God.

THINK IT OUT...

Does Jesus want us to look down on ourselves? Does he want us to think we're worthless? Why is humility so important to God? The more we realize how great God is and how sinful we are, the more humble we'll become. Jesus would never, ever have told someone, "It's important to feel good about yourself." He would have said, "It's important to feel great about your God."

Have you been seeking to be honored? Are you acting good so maybe you can earn brownie points with God, or because you love him? Jesus wanted everyone to know that humility is a mark of a true believer.

LIVE IT OUT...

Jesus said even if you really *do* deserve it, don't sit in the front row. Give up your place in line. Let the other guy cut in front of you on the highway. The bigger they are, the harder they fall. The prouder they are, the more people notice.

"I've deserved this. God owes me. I oughtta pat myself on the back. Feel good about myself. Take pride in myself. See how much I've done? See how great I am?" We might not say it out loud, but we think those things. We like being noticed. And we like to be honored. But God is interested in a humble heart.

God doesn't honor us because of what we do, but because of who we have become through faith in Christ.

PRAY IT OUT...

God, guard me from the desire for applause, either from people or from you. Rather, give me a humble heart. It comes from recognizing my shortcomings and keeping my eyes on your grace instead of my own accomplishments. Pride is subtle! Help me avoid it and always act with humility instead of arrogance. Amen.

32

DECORATING THE HOTEL ROOM

Lisa pounded on the door of her hotel room. It was too tough to dig out the key since she had her hands full.

Inside the room, Maggie was organizing materials for that afternoon's inner-city VBS program. "Who is it?" she called.

"It's me, Lisa!" came the muffled reply. "Open up, I've got my arms full!"

Maggie grunted, slid off the bed, walked across the room and opened up the door.

Lisa stood in front of her with at least half a dozen shopping bags.

"What's all that stuff?" asked Maggie.

"It's for the room," said Lisa, pushing past her friend. "I'm gonna fix this place up just right!"

Maggie stood there staring at her. "What are you talking about? What room?"

"This room! Our hotel room!" replied Lisa, looking around the room affectionately. "All this stuff is for our room. I'm gonna redecorate it!"

"But Lisa! We're here in Baltimore on a mission trip to build houses for low-income families!"

"I know, I know, but it's not gonna hurt anything to take a little time off for ourselves! And besides, if we have to stay here in this drab room, we might as well do all we can to make it look nice."

Lisa set down her bags and began to unload cans of paint, brushes, dropcloths and rags. She had another bag filled with fancy light fixtures and glittery lava lamps for the corners of the room.

Maggie didn't know what to say. "I really don't think it's your job to furnish the hotel room," she told Lisa. But Lisa wouldn't listen.

So that afternoon, when Maggie and the rest of the people from her church went to work on the Habitat for Humanity house, Lisa stayed back at the hotel. "I need to put on another coat of paint as soon as the first one dries," she explained.

They tried to convince her to come. "The whole point of this trip is to serve other people, not just to make yourself more comfortable!" they told her. But she just said she'd be glad to come after the paint had dried and she'd hung up the pictures on the walls.

That night, when Maggie returned to the room, she could hardly recognize it. "You . . . you tore out a wall!" she said.

"Yeah, there just wasn't enough room for the kitchenette I'm installing."

Maggie peered through the opening into the adjoining room. "But Lisa! It's not even your room!"

Lisa sighed. "Look, we're staying here, right?"

Maggie thought for a minute. "Well, yeah, I guess, for the weekend, but then we're heading home and—"

But Lisa just interrupted her. "There you have it," she said. "There is no sense in being uncomfortable for the weekend!"

"But we're going home on Sunday!"

Lisa sighed. "So? Why not do everything we can to enjoy our stay?" Then, she went into the bathroom to move the toilet to the other side of the sink. "It just doesn't look good over there," she said. "Whoever designed this place had no sense of interior decorating, that's for sure!"

And so it went, all weekend. While the other youth group members worked at building homes and leading VBS for the inner-city kids, Lisa stayed in the hotel and decorated her room.

She hung pictures, built another closet, painted, rewired and moved the furniture around.

"This is so cool!" she said, nailing up the bookshelves. "I can't believe what a great job I've done!"

Just then, she heard a knock at the door.

It was Maggie and the rest of the group.

"Hey, what's going on? Why doesn't this door open?" said Maggie, trying to get into the room.

"I had to nail it shut to put up the bookshelf," called Lisa from inside the room.

"What!? Listen, everyone else has checked out and we're loading the van!" called Maggie. "Hurry up and get your things. It's time to go!"

There was only silence from the other side of the door.

"Did you hear me, Lisa? We're leaving!"

"Okay!" came the reply.

"What do you mean, 'okay'? This is it! The trip is over! We're going home! Grab your stuff and let's go!"

Silence again. Then Lisa's voice. "I can't."

"Why not?"

"All my stuff wouldn't fit. Look, you guys have a safe trip! I think I'll just stay here! It's pretty nice in here, and besides, I couldn't get that door open even if I wanted to. I'd have to pull the bookshelf down. Tell everyone at home 'hi' from me!"

Maggie stood there in shock for a full minute. Finally, she just shook her head, sighed and walked down the hallway to the waiting van.

Inside her room, Lisa tidied up a bit, humming quietly to herself. "It's almost the way I want it," she thought. "Just a little more time."

But just as the van pulled away, someone down the hall from Maggie dropped her curling iron on the floor. Lisa didn't even notice the smoke. After all, she'd taken the smoke detector off the ceiling to hang her crystal chandelier.

The fire spread quickly that day, but most people were able to get out in time.

In fact, there was only one casualty.

CHECK IT OUT...

Whenever Jesus talked about priorities, he always encouraged people to think about them from an eternal perspective. Read Matthew 6:19-21 and Mark 8:34-38.

THINK IT OUT...

Where did Jesus say we should store our treasures? How do you store up treasures in Heaven? What kind of things is he talking about? How does it compare to earthly "wealth"? Why is it so easy to store up treasures on earth when we already know we can't keep them?

LIVE IT OUT...

We stay on this earth for only a short time and then comes eternity. It's like a weekend stay at a hotel on the way back home. We're not supposed to get comfortable here; it's not our home.

But most people spend more time getting comfortable here than preparing for the trip home. What about you? Are you slowly cutting the strings that connect you to this world, or are you getting more and more entangled in them? It takes courage to admit you're just passing through this world. Are you willing to do that, or do you just keep stacking furniture against the door in the hopes that you'll never have to check out?

PRAY IT OUT...

God, it's so easy to start getting comfortable here on earth. But this isn't where I'm gonna be spending eternity. Help me remember that I'll be here only for a short time, and while I'm here, my mission is to serve others, not to make myself more comfortable. When it comes time to check out, I wanna come home to be with you in the place you've prepared for me. Amen.

33

THE AMAZING HEALING OF A CHEERLEADER NAMED ANGIE

Angie was the captain of her cheerleading squad. She got straight A's, served as student body president, had perfect teeth and never had a bad hair day. Everyone loved her and respected her. She was even elected Homecoming Queen.

Then, one day she found out she was HIV positive. Angie had AIDS. Immediately the rumors started.

"Did you hear about Angie? Jessie told me she's gay."

"I didn't hear that, but I heard she got it from some guy at camp last summer. I guess they were fooling around. . . ."

"I heard it was from some blood transfusion or something."

Angie's dad did everything he could to help her. He hired the best doctors, flew her to exclusive clinics and paid for the most expensive treatments. It was a good thing he was rich because he spent a fortune. But every specialist and world-renowned expert said the same thing, "I'm sorry. There's nothing we can do. We can slow it down, but we can't stop it."

Then, one of the guys in her homeroom heard about Angie. He called her dad and told him he knew a cure. "There's this guy at our church who's like this faith healer, y'know? I'll bet he could cure Angie. You oughtta call him. His name is Joe."

Well, Angie's dad was skeptical. He didn't put too much stock in miracles. And the thought of having his daughter see some kooky faith healer didn't exactly thrill him.

But he was also desperate. He figured, "What'll it hurt? Nothing else has worked. Maybe this guy could help after all."

So he arranged for a meeting at the guy's church. He brought his checkbook and was ready to offer a giant reward. But Joe didn't even show up! The church secretary mentioned that he'd sent an e-mail earlier that morning. She read it to them: "I've prayed about it and

143

God will heal Angie. All she needs to do is take a shower in the Norskie Motel. That'll do it. No fee."

But Angie and her dad couldn't believe it. "How stupid! Like taking a shower in some cheap hotel is gonna help me!" she said. "All the greatest doctors in the world haven't been able to help me! How is the Norskie Motel's water gonna heal me of AIDS?"

But her friends said, "It's worth a try, isn't it? I mean, if he would have told you to learn some new cheerleading routine, or write an award-winning essay, or be the chairperson of some new club, you'd have jumped at the chance. So what's the big deal about the whole shower thing?"

"It's disgusting! There'll be cockroaches! And the soap won't even be normal size!"

But, finally, they convinced her. She did just as she was told. She checked in, took the shower and even used the itty bitty soap.

And when she walked out of the bathroom, the AIDS was gone. It was unbelievable! No one had ever heard of anything like it before!

Well, you can imagine what happened. Her dad bought the hotel, which was about to go out of business anyway, and started advertising the magical healing waters in Room 115.

Angie was written up in *Time* and *Newsweek* and they even did a special about her on *60 Minutes*. They called it "Angie's Unexplained Spontaneous Remission."

She had some "Healed in Room 115!" T-shirts made up and sold them for $25 a pop. She hired an up-and-coming boy band and toured the country presenting her story of how she'd been healed of AIDS.

People lined up to hear her. They gave her standing ovations. They bought her books and tapes and videos by the truckload.

Of course, she never did meet old Joe. She was so busy she just didn't have the chance to go back and thank him. "He already knows I'm thankful," she thought. "There's no point in bothering to tell him."

Yeah, she's doing pretty well these days. And ol' Joe is still as poor as dirt.

And it doesn't bother him one bit.

CHECK IT OUT...

Healing was an important part of Jesus' ministry. He healed the disabled, blind, deaf, mute and deformed; some had epilepsy, leprosy and other severe illnesses. He cast out demons, raised three people from the dead and healed one guy's amputated ear.

And they responded in different ways. Some followed him, others told their friends, still others danced and shouted and carried on. None of that's really too surprising. But Jesus himself was shocked by the response of the nine men he healed in Luke 17:11-19.

THINK IT OUT...

Jesus asked three questions when the Samaritan returned. Whom do you think he was addressing? Do you think the other men were thankful? Why didn't they return to thank Jesus? How did Jesus feel about their lack of thankfulness?

Even today people respond to Jesus in various ways. Some follow him, others tell their friends, others dance and shout and carry on.

And some just go on with their lives as if nothing happened.

LIVE IT OUT...

Does Jesus still heal people today? Look at what he said in Luke 5:30-32. What sort of healing does he still specialize in?

What healed Angie? The water? The preacher? Notice what healed the Samaritan (Luke 17:19). It's the same thing that heals us: faith. Now, if you've been healed, the question is, whom are you more like— the nine who didn't return with thanksgiving or the one who did?

PRAY IT OUT...

God, lots of times I just go on with my life when miracles happen. I call it chance or circumstance or coincidence. And I forget to come back to you, throw myself at your feet and thank you like the healed Samaritan did. Even when you heal me of the worst disease of all—my sin. Well, today I want to thank you. Thanks for caring about me and knowing the trouble spots in my life . . . the questions that bug me . . . the needs I have. Thanks for faith and thanks for forgiveness. Amen.

34

ONE STRANGE DAY IN THE LOCKER ROOM

It was the weirdest thing he'd ever done, that day Coach Crogan gathered the varsity football team in the locker room. He'd walked in on them while the seniors were all arguing about who should start. Suddenly, he stepped to the front of the room and made them all quiet down.

"All right, men, this is gonna be a tough season but we're gonna survive. I've got an entirely new strategy for this year," he explained.

Then, he whipped out a towel, knelt down and began wiping off the shoes of Alex Becker, the all-state running back.

Everyone was speechless. Coach moved down the line, straightening the socks of his players, cleaning the mud from between their cleats, polishing the leather of their shoes.

Finally, he came to Jay Wallace, the senior captain.

But before Coach could even touch him, Jay leapt to his feet. "Listen, Coach, you can't clean my cleats. It's just not right!"

"If you wanna be a part of this team, you'll let me do this."

"But—"

"If you don't let me clean your cleats, take a hike. There's the door. I don't want to have anything to do with you."

Jay looked around at the other players. No one moved. Finally, Jay said, "All right, man—if it's that important, don't stop at my cleats—you can do a few loads of my laundry as well!" Some of the other players held their noses. They'd smelled Jay's laundry.

"The shoes are enough for now," Coach said.

When he finished, he tossed the grimy towel aside and announced, "Now, go and do likewise."

After he left the locker room, the players all thought he'd gone off the deep end. Maybe he'd been teaching tackling techniques without a helmet again. They all shook their heads and went home.

And that night, on his way home from practice, Coach Crogan's car was struck head-on by a semi. He was killed instantly. The semi driver walked away without a scratch. Everyone was shocked. No one in the community could believe that Coach Crogan was dead.

The Pep Club posted his photo next to the trophy case and, for the rest of the season, the team wore black armbands in memory of their coach. They dedicated each game to Coach Crogan. And they played like pros. They were inspired. The walls of the locker room were covered with sayings like, "Slay the Buccaneers," "Step on the Stingrays," "Ground the Falcons," "Crush the Weasels." And that's just what they did. Game after game. They were on fire.

Of course, they put the whole cleat-cleaning thing out of their minds. After all, he couldn't have really meant what he said: *"Go and do likewise!"* That's ridiculous! Who ever heard of cleaning out the other team's cleats before the game? How could you win with that kind of an attitude? How could you beat someone you were kneeling to serve?

They had a great year that year Coach Crogan died. They made it all the way to the state playoffs. Folks said it was the best team they'd ever had in that town.

Within a few years, most of the players had forgotten that day in the locker room when their coach pulled out a towel and cleaned their cleats. But everywhere they went, they were glad to tell people about the way they almost beat Central High in the playoffs. How they almost made it to state. Almost.

And with each passing year, fewer and fewer people knew whose picture that was in the corner of the gym by the trophy case. Just gathering dust.

CHECK IT OUT...

Sometimes Jesus didn't just tell a parable, he acted one out. Does this story sound familiar? It should after you read John 13:1-17.

THINK IT OUT...

How would you feel if a teacher or coach knelt to clean out your toe jam? What would happen if a football team took Jesus' words literally? Would cleat-cleaning really change the outcome of the game?

Would it change *anything*?

Following Jesus requires a radical change. Rather than relying on our own common sense we need to start thinking like Jesus did. And he came to serve people, no matter what it cost him.

How *can* you beat someone you're kneeling to serve? Is it possible to have the attitude Jesus was talking about? Why is it so hard to have that attitude when we're in competition? What do you think Jesus *really* meant when he said, "Go and do likewise"?

LIVE IT OUT...

It was quite a reversal for Jesus to clean the feet of his followers—that was normally the job of a servant . . . a servant? . . . aha.

Jesus told his followers they should follow his example and act in the same way, by humbly serving others. It's a reversal. Not what you'd expect. And following the example of Jesus means serving others, too—even when it isn't the most glamorous job in the world. Even when it means doing something no one else would expect.

Think about your life. Consider the people you know at school. In church. Where you work. Whose feet need washing? Are you willing to do it? If not you, who? If not now, when?

PRAY IT OUT...

Dear God, I want to follow Jesus all the way. Show me what it means to "wash the feet" of other people. Help me to humbly serve them. Even if it means doing stuff that isn't what people in the world would normally do. To kneel in humility and serve with authenticity. Even if it seems a little weird. Help me follow your example and live the great reversal in practical ways. All the way. Every day. Amen.

35

GUESS WHAT I GOT IN MY GARAGE?

Seagulls called overhead as Greg and Andy approached the garage door. "Wait 'til you see what I've got in here!" said Greg. Andy heard him, but he couldn't help but glance past his friend toward the bay. Several sailboats were already on the water.

Greg reached down and dramatically yanked open the door.

Inside the garage was a mint-condition, two-year-old, Porsche 911 Carrera.

"Whoa!" said Andy. "I don't believe it! What a beauty!" He walked over and ran his hand along the shiny, smooth exterior.

Greg grinned. "Yeah, Dad handed the keys over to me a couple years ago and told me she's all mine to drive. I can take her out anytime I want!"

Andy opened the door to the passenger seat and eased down onto the genuine leather seat. "Well, hey! Let's take her for a spin!"

Greg gasped. "What, are you nuts? I've never taken this thing out of the garage!"

Andy couldn't believe it! "Why not?"

"What if I damaged it or something? Can you imagine what my dad would do if I brought it back with a dent in the side?"

"I don't know, I mean, wear and tear—it happens."

"Not to a Porsche!"

"Well, what's the good of having a Porsche if you never drive it?"

"I can show it to people like you when they come visit."

Andy just shook his head. "I don't get it. . . ."

"C'mere," said Greg. "I've got something else I gotta show you." He led Andy back into the house and upstairs to a room with eight locks on the door. One by one he unlocked them and finally, swung the door open.

"Look over there in the corner," he said.

Andy gazed in the corner of the room. There, in the dim light on a little backlit platform was a stack of several dozen bricks of gold bullion.

"Is that real gold?" Andy gasped.

"Of course. And there's a lot more where that came from. Dad gave it to me last year."

"Man, your dad's generous! If you invested this on Wall Street, you could make a fortune!" said Andy.

Greg sighed. "You just don't get it, do you? You take a risk anytime you invest in something. What if it goes belly up? What if you end up losing money instead of gaining returns? It's not my gold to use—"

"But I thought you said your dad gave it to you?"

"Well, yeah he did. He said I could buy anything I want with it. But I *never* use any of the stuff Dad gives me. I just *store* it."

Andy walked over and looked at the pile of gold that his friend would never spend. "So what do you do with all this gold if you don't invest it?"

"I polish it. Sometimes I build little towers and then knock 'em down again. Dad gives me all kinds of stuff. Why, just last week he gave me a tuba!"

"Wow! Where is it?"

"I buried it out there in the sand. Wouldn't want to lose it or anything. Anyway, what about you? Do you have any cool stuff?"

"Oh, not really. Nothing like you. I mean, I'm taking out my dad's sailboat this afternoon, but that's about it. He let's me use it on the weekends. Hey, wanna come along?"

"Naw," said Greg. "I've gotta wax the car. But thanks for the invitation."

Andy and Greg walked back outside and Andy gazed at the waves lapping at the shore of the bay. "Sure you don't wanna come?"

"Yeah. I'll see you on Monday."

Andy nodded and walked toward the marina.

Greg went inside the garage and spent the next hour waxing his Porsche. "Won't Dad be proud!" he thought. Then he flipped off the light, closed the garage door and locked it. "No one's gonna steal that thing!" he said, smiling.

Meanwhile, Andy arrived at the sailboat. He untied it from the dock and peered out across the bay. "Looks like a nice brisk breeze out there, just past the peninsula," he thought.

It didn't take him long to maneuver the boat out of the harbor. That's when the wind really picked up. The sails billowed out and the boat began to pick up speed.

Wind tossed back his hair and spray pelted his face. "It's great to be on the water again!" he yelled. "Thanks, Dad!"

He passed the breakers near the peninsula and trimmed the sails. "Well, this is it! No turning back now!" he thought. "With a breeze like this, there's no telling how far I can go!"

Then, he pointed the sailboat toward the open water, and headed out to sea.

CHECK IT OUT...

Read Matthew 25:14-30. The point of this story is simple: use it or lose it.

We're not owners, just caretakers. The talents aren't ours, they're God's, lent to us for a little while. But he doesn't want us to sit on them.

THINK IT OUT...

When Jesus explained a similar story, he said, "From everyone who has been given much, much will be demanded; and from the one who has been entrusted with much, much more will be asked" (Luke 12:48). Have you been given much? What does God want you do to with it?

In his heart of hearts, God is a gift-giver. He can't help it. That's what love does. So what do we do with the gifts he hands over to us? We lock them up. We hide them. We bury them. Because we might get laughed at. Or rejected.

And God's gifts to us remain unopened, gathering dust in a forgotten corner of our souls. All because we're ashamed of the talents or abilities or genius God has given us. What gifts has he handed to you? Playing the trumpet? Writing? Acting? Listening? What are you doing with them?

LIVE IT OUT...

God loves to take chances. He's a risk-taker. He'd rather we risk all in following him than hold back and be "safe." You gotta risk a little if you want to get anywhere. He honors those who take chances for him. Are you willing to do it? What kind of risk is God asking you to take in his name today? Will you take your gifts out of storage and risk everything for God on the open water?

PRAY IT OUT...

God, your gifts to us are meant to be used, not locked away. I don't wanna pace myself. I don't wanna hold anything back. I wanna taste the salty spray as I venture beyond the bay. Out of the harbor. Fill my sails, Spirit! Send me out to sea, far beyond my safety zone. No turning back. All of my gifts. All of myself. All for you, all of the time. That's where the adventure of serving you begins. Amen.

36

THE ONLY WAY TO KILL A VAMPIRE

Regis galloped toward the castle. From the nearby woods he could hear fanged beasts howling and crashing toward him through the mist-enshrouded underbrush. Yet he rode on. Nothing was going to stop him. He was there to save Brittany, his fiancée. She'd been lured here. Deceived by the Lord of Darkness. But Regis had faced vampires before. He knew what he had to do.

Finally, the fog parted slightly, and the formidable stone walls of the vampire's fortress rose before him. The crooked pathway ahead was too narrow for his horse. He would have to travel the rest of the way on foot.

He grabbed his saddle bag and tethered his horse. "I'll be back," he whispered, patting her on the head.

She snorted and began clawing at the ground.

"I promise."

Regis turned and ascended the long winding path toward the towering gray structure.

Once inside the gloomy halls, he could hear the echoes of screams from deep inside the dungeon. *So,* he thought to himself, *Brittany's not the only one here. Well, first thing's first.*

Before he could save them, he needed to face the monster. Otherwise, it would still have power over them all. He had to stop the vampire. And the only way to stop him was to destroy him.

The corridor ended in a large banquet room where a feast lay spread across the table. Long flickering torches lined the walls and threw eerie shadows around the room.

Suddenly, he heard a voice, "Care to join me for a bite to eat before the big finale?" The vampire stepped out of the shadows and held up a glass of wine. A smile curled across his face.

He didn't look very frightening. An elegant black cape draped across his lanky frame and fluttered gently behind him as he walked. His smile seemed sincere. He was handsome and walked with an air of nobility.

But his eyes gave him away. He had the cold, dark eyes of a snake.

"So, it's you," said Regis, reaching into his bag. "I should have expected as much."

"Yes, my old friend," hissed the vampire. "It's me."

They'd faced each other before. They'd even been friends, long ago. So long ago it seemed like it'd been in another life. Regis just shook his head. "We used to play together when we were kids. What happened? Why did you choose the darkness over the light?"

The vampire smiled, revealing his menacing teeth. "The darkness is more powerful."

"I beg to differ," said Regis. "Now, I know she's here and I won't return home without her."

"Then you won't return home at all!" laughed the vampire. He took a sip of his wine and walked over to the table. "She's mine now, Regis. She chose to come here. I didn't force her."

"You enticed her!"

"I *charmed* her," he said quickly. "Look here. . . ." He picked something up from the table. "Recognize this?"

It was the engagement ring Regis had bought Brittany last month.

"Where did you get that?" he yelled.

"She took it off. She was going to throw it away, but then she gave it to me." He turned it in his fingers, gazing at the gem in the flickering light. "Very elegant, my old friend. I'm impressed with your taste. . . ." Then he set it down and motioned toward the table. "Now, let's have a bite to eat. What do you say?"

Regis clutched the wooden stake and hammer. "I'm not hungry," he said. "Where is Brittany? What've you done to her?"

The vampire sighed. "Cliché. Cliché. Cliché. She's in my chambers. . . . Come, now, Regis. Join me. Become one of us. Stop fighting the inevitable. If you join me, you can be with Brittany again."

"If I destroy you, I set her free."

Regis had approached to within a few feet of the vampire. The vampire pushed his chair away from the table and leaped to his feet. In a split-second his face changed as his true nature took over. It was a ghastly transformation.

His eyes narrowed and became slits in his leathery face. His handsome features faded and he parted his blood-red lips to reveal razor-sharp teeth. He pulled out two daggers from a sash around his waist.

In a moment he was standing on the table. The next he was on the ceiling, laughing coldly. "Follow me, my friend!" The vampire spat out the words and then whipped his cloak around himself in a flurry of darkness and mist. A shadow swallowed him and nothing remained but a pool of liquid darkness that slithered across the ceiling and then shot across the room toward the stairs.

Regis snatched a torch from the wall and ran toward the stairwell. He threw open the door.

Darkness.

He paused for a moment before stepping forward. He knew the vampire could change into any form at will. A bat. A snake. A wolf. He looked around.

Nothing.

Slowly, he stepped forward and as he did, he felt the hot breath of his adversary on the back of his neck. The creature was on the wall above the door! He spun around and waved the flame at the beast's face. It fell upon him, trying to shove him down the stairs. But Regis was agile and ducked away.

As the vampire slashed toward him with one of his daggers, Regis raised the stake.

The vampire stared at Regis and said, "I give you my riddle. Solve it and live; otherwise die," and without awaiting a reply, he said,

"The more you think you have, the less you really own.
Those with more don't know it, those with less are known."

Regis smiled, "The answer is . . . humility." And he brought the hammer down.

With a screech, the vampire clawed at the stake with his hands. "No!" he cried. "I will not die today!"

But Regis was quick. He slammed the hammer down again and again, driving the stake not only through the creature's heart, but right out his back. And the dark, caped figure crumpled to the ground.

Regis glanced around the castle. Back in the banquet room, all the food on the table was turning rotten and old. Mold and maggots covered everything and worms dripped onto the ground.

Yet, darkness had begun to fade and light was seeping through the cracks in the walls. As the cracks enlarged, the stone fortress began to crumble. *I better hurry,* he thought to himself, *before it's too late to save Brittany!*

He looked where the vampire's body had fallen. Nothing but a pile of sooty black clothes and a chain full of keys. Regis snatched them up and descended into the heart of the dungeon.

Lining the walls on either side were cells packed with prisoners. People from all over the countryside were locked inside. As Regis ran to each cell, he recognized many of the faces. "Come on out! Hurry up! You're free!" he yelled as he threw open the doors to their cells.

One by one, they began to stumble out. Regis pointed them toward the castle's entrance. "Hurry! I'll be with you in a little bit!" he yelled. And off they ran.

But the strangest thing of all was this: Many chose to remain in their cells. "The vampire has always taken good care of us," they said without looking up. "I'm sure he'll continue to feed us from his bountiful table."

"I doubt the cell has really been opened," said others, "I'll just stay here until I am convinced."

"I'm too busy to leave," said some while rearranging rocks on the floor of their cells, "maybe later."

"No!" cried Regis. "There's no time to waste! Hurry!"

But they chose to remain. And what could he do? He'd set them free. He couldn't force them to follow him to safety.

Regis had many cells to open and the ceiling was crumbling all around him. He'd opened dozens of doors, but still, he had not found Brittany.

He ran forward, dodging rocks and boulders and crumbled stones. The entire castle was beginning to sink into the mountainside.

At the end of the hallway he found a huge metal door. He had only one key left, and it fit the lock, but the door remained shut. He called inside and hammered on the door with his fists, "Brittany? Are you in there? It's me, Regis!"

From deep inside he heard the voice of his dearest love. "Regis? Is that you?"

"Yes!"

"You came for me? But I failed you! I betrayed you! I left you for him!" she cried.

"I forgive you!" called Regis. "Now, try the door from the inside! We must hurry!"

Slowly, the door creaked and burst open.

Regis threw his arms around her and then grabbed her hand. "C'mon," he yelled. "I know the way out!"

Amidst the falling rocks and stones, Regis and Brittany ran through the corridors, back up the stairs and outside to safety. As they neared Regis's horse, the vampire's castle crumbled to the ground and was swallowed by the hillside behind them. All around them, the sky was alive with light. Dawn had finally arrived.

Suddenly, Brittany turned to Regis. "My ring is gone."

"You gave it to him," said Regis.

And then she lowered her eyes. "I . . . I gave everything to him."

"I know," said Regis.

"But you still came," she whispered. "Why?"

"I made you a promise that I'd always be there for you."

"But how did you beat him? He had the power to kill you! Nothing is stronger than death!"

"There's one thing stronger." he said. "Love. My love for you."

"But didn't the vampire also love me?" she asked, bewildered.

"No, he *wanted* you. But I *loved* you. That's why I came."

She threw her arms around him. And he brushed his hand across her cheek. "I have one more question. Will you truly marry me?"

"Oh, yes," she whispered.

"No more crying now, it's time to celebrate," he said. "C'mon. We're still a long way from home. And I have a feeling we haven't seen the last of that vampire. Just stick by my side and you'll be safe."

He lifted her onto his horse, and they galloped toward home.

CHECK IT OUT...

Think of a vampire and you'll have a good idea what Satan is like. Always seeking souls to imprison and enslave. Bloodthirsty. Evil. Murderous. Selfish. Proud, vicious and cruel.

The religious leaders of Jesus' day accused him of working for the Prince of Darkness. Look at Jesus' response in Luke 11:20-22.

THINK IT OUT...

In the story, some people chose to remain in the castle. Why? Did they have good reasons? What happened to them as a result? Do people respond that way to Jesus today?

What about the vampire . . . how does the media today portray Satan? How do they portray Jesus? Which of them do they seem to think is stronger? Where did they get that idea?

LIVE IT OUT...

The only way to kill a vampire is to send in someone stronger who has the right tools to put him out of action. Jesus did.

Jesus conquered not only the devil, but death itself. He let Satan sink his fangs in. While hanging on the cross, Jesus felt the venom of evil fill his veins. He took all our sins upon himself and suffered in our place. But he was stronger than sin, death and the devil.

And he still is.

Jesus is stronger than any other power. No matter what you need deliverance from, he can do it. Ask him to, right now.

PRAY IT OUT...

Dear Jesus, I need rescuing. I've sold out and slept with the enemy. Forgive me! Sometimes, even though you've opened the door, I'm tempted to linger in my cell. You bring freedom for every area of life. Show me that love today. Free me from the addictions to evil that seem so charming. I want to follow you, step by step, all the way home. Amen.

TOPICAL INDEX:

Scripture Index: